PARENTS AS ADVOCATES

Liz Dempsey Lee

PARENTS AS ADVOCATES

Supporting K-12 students and their families across identities

The Education Studies Collection

Collection editor
Dr Janise Hurtig

First published in 2023 by Lived Places Publishing

All rights reserved. No part of this publication may be reproduced, stored in a retrieval system, or transmitted in any form or by any means, electronic, mechanical, photocopying, recording or otherwise, without prior permission in writing from the publisher.

The authors and editors have made every effort to ensure the accuracy of information contained in this publication, but assume no responsibility for any errors, inaccuracies, inconsistencies and omissions. Likewise, every effort has been made to contact copyright holders. If any copyright material has been reproduced unwittingly and without permission the Publisher will gladly receive information enabling them to rectify any error or omission in subsequent editions.

Copyright © 2023 Lived Places Publishing

British Library Cataloguing in Publication Data

A CIP record for this book is available from the British Library

ISBN: 9781915271600 (pbk)

ISBN: 9781915271617 (ePDF)

ISBN: 9781915271624 (ePUB)

The right of Liz Dempsey Lee to be identified as the Author of this work has been asserted by them in accordance with the Copyright, Design and Patents Act 1988.

Cover design by Fiachra McCarthy

Book design by Rachel Trolove of Twin Trail Design

Typeset by Newgen Publishing UK

Lived Places Publishing

Long Island

New York 11789

www.livedplacespublishing.com

To my family—mom and dad—for all the support and love, Amelia, Abby, and James—for the laughter and fun, Jodi—for having faith in me, and Chris—none of this would be possible without you. I am full of love.

Author's Note

All names in this book are pseudonyms and identifying details have been changed to protect anonymity.

Abstract

The family-school relationship is central to a child's education, and research demonstrates that family engagement can lead to better educational outcomes for students. No matter how well-prepared educators are, to meet the needs of their students and families, interpersonal conflict and parent advocacy are normal and expected parts of the family-school relationship.

Schools in the United States serve students from many, and overlapping, social identities. Each family's specific social identities shift the ways in which they interact with their child's school, and, the more educators understand about their students and families, the better they can support them.

Key words

Parent advocacy
Family-school relationship
Family engagement
Race and parent advocacy
Ability and parent advocacy
Gender identity and parent advocacy
High socioeconomic status and parent advocacy

Contents

Learning objectives	xiii
Introduction	1
Chapter 1 Race and ethnicity	21
Chapter 2 Ability	43
Chapter 3 Gender identity	65
Chapter 4 High socioeconomic status	91
Conclusion	113
References	119
Index	131

Learning objectives

1. Family (or child) social identities are critical aspects which inform how and why parents advocate.
2. Developing understanding of family (or child) social identities results in more compassionate and informed responses to parent concerns.
3. Developing understanding of family (or child) social identities results in deeper and stronger family-school relationships.
4. Compassion, informed responses, and better family-school relationships lead to better outcomes for children.

Introduction

"Now you try."

Chapter learning objectives

To gain a deeper understanding of how context influences the family-school relationship and parent advocacy.

Genesis of book

As an early career teacher, I taught in a small northeastern city—a former mill town that had never quite recovered from the economic blow of the mill closing. The poverty rate was high, as was unemployment. I oversaw a Title 1 funded kindergarten classroom focused on boosting student literacy. Each day, selected students would attend their regular half-day class and come to me for the other half of the day. In the beginning-of-year literacy assessments, my students fared poorly. None knew all their letters. Some had never held a pencil, and others could not orient a book to an upright, left to right position. And so, we worked intensely to address these early literacy concepts. I worked with students' families as well, teaching them about the value of reading to children and providing activities and books to use at home.

Ideally, my classroom would increase student skills in a short amount of time and transition them out of my classroom.

However, this assumed that the primary obstacle my students faced was a lack of experience and exposure. Of course, this was not always the case. Many students had complicated situations. Dylan[1] qualified for free and reduced meals and would eat daily as much food as the food service workers gave him—up to three meals at breakfast and also at lunch. Victoria didn't speak—at all. Donny arrived in the classroom each morning and promptly fell asleep in the book corner. And Kelli played out the same scenario in the play kitchen day after day. "Hide the babies in the closet! The police are coming!"

But of all these children, Dallas stood out. A quiet redhead with a smattering of freckles across his pale face, he worked hard in class. He entered kindergarten recognizing only one letter, the first letter of his name. He and I worked and worked, but any gains made during the week were erased over the weekend and on Monday we were back at the beginning. No matter which approaches I used, letters simply didn't stick in Dallas's mind. Something else was going on.

His parents, Joe and Gail, whom I had never met, were due for their first parent literacy engagement meeting. When they arrived, I shared my concerns and explained that they could support Dallas at home, and I was happy to teach them how. Thanks to a generous grant, I had books and activities for Dallas to keep. I modeled reading a picture book to an early reader and carefully explained how to engage Dallas, where to pause, and how often they should read together.

I turned to Joe and handed him the book saying, "Here, now you try!" He looked at the book as if it were a rattlesnake and reluctantly opened it. Oblivious, I nattered on about the joy of books and invited him to start reading—an impossible request, as it turned out, because Joe was unable to read. At this moment, the weight of my faulty assumptions fell squarely onto us all—and that weight broke our relationship. Joe and Gail were deeply embarrassed. Without a word, they got up and left as quickly as they could. I never saw them again. They didn't come to conferences, parties, or school events. By the end of the year, I suspected that Dallas had a serious learning disability and that perhaps his father did as well. My one-size-fits-all approach to working with parents had cut Dallas's greatest advocates, those who knew him best, from participating in his education. This was, of course, not deliberate, but the consequences were severe and lasting, nonetheless.

Fast forward to summer 2019, when I began my dissertation research on perceptions of education among parents with different socioeconomic backgrounds. As I worked, I had Dallas, Joe, and Gail in my mind. That summer, I spoke with many parents both for my research and in the course of my daily life as a parent to three young children. I sat across from Ada, a mother of two, and listened as she "described a systematic bullying campaign lasting two school years" (Lee, 2020, p. 124). Although the reasons for this bullying were not entirely obvious, her classmates did reference her Middle Eastern heritage, asking "do you belong to ISIS?" (Lee, 2020, p. 120). Ada advocated tirelessly for her daughter with little effect. The bullying did not end until her daughter transitioned to high school.

Just a day before I met Ada, I'd had a long conversation with another parent, Mandy (not part of my research). Mandy was a typical parent in her community—she was white, had an MBA, and worked at a financial services firm in the nearby city. Together, she and her husband made a comfortable living in a town where the median price for a house was $900,000. Mandy was deep in anxiety over math instruction at her daughter's school. In this mother's view, her third grader was quite advanced in math and, in her view, the conceptual mathematics program in her public elementary school was not challenging enough. She had spoken with the teacher, who disagreed. I did not know enough about either her daughter or the school to be able to evaluate Mandy's statement; however, I was struck by the meaning she pulled from this situation. Mandy believed that without a more rigorous—and by this she meant traditional—teaching style, her daughter's future would be ruined. She would never be accepted to a decent college, and that would have lifelong negative consequences. So, Mandy outlined a three-point plan to remediate this perceived weakness of the school:

1. Lobby the school to adopt a more "rigorous" curriculum, as defined by her.
2. Lobby the school to provide more advanced and traditional teaching to her child in addition to the regular class work.
3. Pay thousands of dollars for a traditionally structured, extra after-school math class twice a week for her daughter.

Mandy posted her concerns on social media and, within a week, had garnered more than 100 signatures on a petition. By the next week she had organized 25 parents to speak at the school board meeting and secured a meeting with the district superintendent.

Ada's and Mandy's children attended schools in the same community but had very different experiences. Ada's child was bullied every day. So, Ada had immediate and pressing concerns.

The other child appeared to be thriving, but her mother, Mandy, had deep-seated concerns—not about her daughter's present circumstances, but about a hypothetical problem located more than ten years in the future. Likewise, both parents received different responses to their advocacy. Ada was ultimately unsuccessful in addressing her concern, while Mandy was rapidly heard by the broader community of parents, the school board, and the superintendent. I wanted to understand how a family's social identity might influence different views of education, the ways parents advocate for their students, and different outcomes (Lee, 2020).

Parent advocacy

This book is an in-depth exploration of a critical facet of teachers' work with students' families—*parent advocacy*. Each chapter explores a distinct characteristic that influences parent advocacy: race and ethnicity, ability, gender identity, and high socioeconomic status. Parent advocacy is defined as actions taken by a parent in support of their student, with the goal of influencing the educational setting to best meet the perceived educational, social, and/or emotional needs of the child. Like the desire to engage with schools, parent advocacy emerges from a place of concern and love for children. Moreover, parents advocate for many different reasons and in different ways, depending on their and their student's needs as defined by that family's context.

As we see in the examples of Joe, Ada, and Mandy, not all parent advocacy involves problems of equal weight. All parents' concerns should be evaluated by educators with attention to the family's social identity and how that interconnects with the larger settings of school and community. Of these three parents, Joe was completely excluded from his child's learning and was rendered voiceless. Mandy was worried about her child's distant future, while Ada struggled with a substantial and immediate problem faced by her child. These parents had remarkably different experiences advocating.

This book is based on my mixed methods dissertation research, titled *Win the Game or Build Decent Humans? Parental Perceptions of the Family School-Relationship Across Socioeconomic Backgrounds* (Lee, 2020). I also draw extensively on my own experiences and observations as an early childhood educator and parent to three. My research centered on two primary questions. "Does socioeconomic status influence perceptions of engagement among parents in high-income public schools?" focused the quantitative section (Lee, 2020, p. 78). The qualitative section asked, "How do parents of children in a high-income public-school system describe their relationship with the school?" The related sub-questions asked "To what do they attribute their experiences (positive, negative, neutral)?," and "Do their perceptions vary by socioeconomic status?" (Lee, 2020, p. 79).

This book extends that work by focusing on the intersection of families, schools, parent advocacy, and social identity. We'll explore how social identity influences parent advocacy and how educators and school staff can develop awareness of these issues and pivot educational practices to support the needs of all students. Before we get started, we need to outline a few key ideas. How do we define family? Who do we serve in our classrooms? What is a social identity? Understanding more about the families we work with is critical to building a strong family-school relationship, to successfully navigating parent advocacy, and doing so in a way that creates the best outcomes for students.

Getting started: American families

What is a family?

Close your eyes and picture a family. Perhaps you pictured your own family arrangement or those of your friends and neighbors. Perhaps your family resembled that of Joe, Ada, or Mandy. Or perhaps your experiences of family look quite different. Until relatively recently in the United States, media often depicted families as nuclear, white, suburban, middle-class, and living in their own home, complete with the "white picket fence." This vision of family has been expanded upon and overwritten by the variety and visibility of real-world, contemporary families. However, this outdated viewpoint still exists and holds sway with some Americans, as evidenced by local and state level battles over what can be taught in schools. Consequently, educators should have a toolbox that allows them to successfully work with diverse families and to articulate the benefits of doing so to those who lack understanding.

In this book, we define "family" as a group living together and caring for each other. Connections can be biological, legal (marriage or adoption), or social and emotional (developed through cohabitation). "Parent" is used in this book as shorthand to describe all types of primary caregivers, including but not limited to legal guardians, aunts and uncles, and grandparents. Before exploring these ideas and constructs in depth, let's begin with an overview of the nature and diversity of families and children in the contemporary United States.

Families—race and ethnicity

American families increasingly reflect the world. Our students and families come from many places around the globe, they are increasingly diverse by race and ethnicity, speak many languages, and reflect a variety of abilities, gender identities, sexual orientations, and incomes. As of 2021, in the United States there were nearly 50 million students enrolled in PreK-12 public schools (NCES). The racial breakdown of residents in the United States shows that people who are white still make up the majority in the United States at 64.1 percent of the population (Jones et al., 2021). However, according to the 2020 Census, among children (0–17) in the United States, 53 percent identify as white (Jones et al., 2021).

This pattern of increasing racial and ethnic diversity is especially visible among children. For example, Jones et al. (2021) document that Black American adults comprise 12 percent of the population, while Black children comprise 13.9 percent; Hispanic adults constitute 16.8 percent of the adult population, while Hispanic children constitute 25.7 percent. Moreover, the authors indicate that between 2010 and 2020, the percentage of people identifying as bi- or multiracial increased from 2.9 to 10.2 percent. US K-12 students are more racially and ethnically diverse than ever before.

Families and ability

Across the globe, more than 240 million children have been diagnosed with educational needs which require special approaches to education. This amounts to roughly one of every ten children, worldwide, requiring education which specifically meets their needs; unsurprisingly, these children "face multiple and compounding challenges in realizing their rights" (UNICEF, 2021). In the United States alone, approximately 7.2 million children were identified as having a disability and received services in the 2020–2021 school years (NCES, 2022).

In the United States, the most common diagnoses receiving support fall into the category of "specific learning disability" which includes diagnoses such as dyslexia and dyscalculia (NCES, 2022). This category accounts for 30–35 percent of students receiving special education in the United States (NCES, 2022). In many countries, including the United States, schools are mandated to provide education to all children regardless of need. Teachers connect with many families with children with needs over their career. These students have a broad range of diagnoses which intersect with other family and student characteristics.

Families with transgender or nonbinary children

Accurate numbers regarding LGBTQ+ children are hard to find because in many parts of the United States it remains dangerous to identify as queer. This is particularly true for those who are transgender or nonbinary. However, according to the Williams Institute (n.d.), among adults between ages 18 and 60, approximately 1.2 million, or roughly 11 percent of all LGBTQ+

adults, identify as nonbinary. Among all children aged 13–17, close to 1 percent identify as transgender, while about 9.54 percent of all LGBTQ+ children 13–17 identify as transgender. Lastly, 26 percent of LGBTQ+ youth identify as nonbinary (Williams Institute, 2022).

Families—socioeconomic status

Likewise, families vary significantly in the resources available to them. In 2021, the median household income in the United States was $69,717 (Guzman, 2022) and the US poverty level was 12.8 percent of all residents (Benson, 2022). In the United States, poverty is defined as anyone living below the poverty threshold which, in 2022, was $27,750 for a family of four (ASPE, n.d.). Any family of four earning less than this amount is determined to be poor. Therefore, more than one in ten of all Americans is considered to be living in poverty by the United States government. This number increases when we consider only numbers of children living in poverty. In 2021, the child poverty rate was 15.3 percent; in other words, of all people under age 18 in the United States, fifteen out of every hundred live in poverty (Creamer et al., 2022).

Across the country, 70.1 percent of children live in households with two parents, although these parents are not necessarily married; 25.8 percent of children live in single-parent households and, of these, the vast majority (21.4 percent) reside with their mother. The remaining 4.4 percent reside with their father. An additional 4 per cent of children live with neither parent, instead residing with someone beyond the immediate family, such as a grandparent (Anderson, Hemez, and Kreider, 2022).

Social identities and biases

The term social identity can be defined as "the part of self-concept that is derived from memberships in social groups or categories, ranging from family to nationality or race" (APA Dictionary). A family's social identity can influence the family-school relationship because social identities influence both how a family interacts with a school and how educators perceive families. These differences are not related to the individual personalities of a parent or educator but, instead, tap into common biases in society. These biases are so well established and so common that they are rendered nearly invisible, and they form the foundation of institutional practices. Institutional biases are the "practices, scripts, or procedures that work to systematically give advantage to certain groups or agendas over others. Institutionalized bias is built into the fabric of institutions" (Lucas).

The experience of Dallas's father illustrates the impact of social identities on the family-school relationship. His potential learning disability was a poor match for an institution which operates on the written word. Not only did his inability to read put him at a disadvantage, but Joe's disability also was rendered invisible to school staff. Mandy's social identity was that of high socioeconomic status. She had resources including connections on social media to mobilize parents, and within a month she was in front of the educational decision makers with her concerns. Joe's social identity impeded his ability to advocate, while Mandy's enhanced hers.

These biases often center on social identities, for example, racism, ableism, gender identity, and income. For example, racial biases have well known negative impacts on education (Gandara and

Contreras, 2009; Rothstein, 2004; Shapiro, 2004). Likewise, family income, especially when families have disposable income, also affects the family-school relationship(Cheadle and Amato, 2011; Dumais, Kessinger, and Ghosh, 2012; Hill and Taylor, 2004; Lareau and Shumar, 1996; Robinson and Harris, 2014).

Gender differences between men and women provide one common example of bias at work in education especially as it pertains to parent advocacy. In my dissertation (Lee, 2020), I conducted seven in-depth parent interviews. These parents all lived in similar high-income, predominately white communities. Of the seven, two were white, married, cisgender men in households with family incomes of more than double their state's average. They described participating in their child's education with ease. In fact, both men reported also being sought out and asked for their views and *invited* to take on multiple leadership roles. One concluded that being included was simple because "they will take parents off the street. I simply had to raise my hand and say I'm interested" (Lee, 2020, p. 129).

However, for the two married, cisgender white women among the seven, both also in families with high income, it was more challenging to have their advocacy heard. Both mothers advocated for their children, and both were initially rebuffed. They both also subsequently employed pressure and leveraged personal support systems "to sharpen and deliver their messages" (Lee, 2020, p. 127). Eventually they persevered—essentially coming to a rapprochement with their child's school administration.

Finally, race, resources, and marital status matter as well. The final three parents I interviewed were single mothers of color or single white mothers with children of color. All earned less than half of their area's median income. They all reported being dismissed with regularity. When one mother missed Back-to-School Night because she did not have a babysitter, she asked to meet with the teachers and "they declined" (Lee, 2020, p. 129). By necessity, these mothers' approaches to advocacy departed from what the school community expected. Although this is a small sample, it illustrates that parent advocacy and engagement are decidedly different from family to family. In these examples alone, approaches vary from uncomplicated—"I simply had to raise my hand and say I'm interested and then show up"—to challenging—"I was asking to meet with the teachers, and they declined" (Lee, 2020, p. 129).

Families have more than one social identity, and these multiple identities interact in complicated ways. Joe not only had a learning issue, but his family was also considered to be low-income. These two particular identities created a quandary for him. Reading is important to employment. Income is important to diagnosing and managing disabilities. Joe was stuck. Without the ability to read, he was less likely to get a higher paying job with benefits. Without a higher paying job and benefits, he was less likely to get the supports he needed to learn to read. Mandy also had multiple social identities. For example, she was both white and high-income. She was able to combine her connections, financial resources, and her ease in navigating institutions to draw attention to her concerns. Community expectations play a role in parent advocacy, in part, because not all parents fit easily into the expectations of educators.

The "good parent"

Context is an essential component in the stories of Joe, Ada, and Mandy. Every parent and child exist within the larger context of their school and community. For many reasons, some parents and children are more in step with school and community expectations than others. For this reason, the assumptions and expectations which emerge from the social identities of educators play an equally important role. They also influence the family-school relationship, parent advocacy, and a child's school experience. Our social identities determine how we navigate the classroom, interact with families, and respond to challenging situations. My own story illustrates this idea. I am a white woman and I grew up in a middle-income community, which was predominately white and Catholic.

In fact, it wasn't until college that I realized that most people weren't Irish-Catholic. In my childhood, every adult could read, and if you were struggling, you had the resources needed to figure it out. I had never met an adult unable to read—and I even judged parents who did not read with their children at home. I gave no thought to why this might be. In my mind, good parents read with their kids. If you didn't, I assumed you weren't a good parent. Such was my overly simplistic view.

The "good" parent is an image of parenting to which families must "conform" in order to be taken seriously (Dyrness, 2011, p. 109). It is also the standard by which all parents are judged. As educators, we make many subconscious judgments about the families we serve, as I did with Joe. We take in a child's clothing, cleanliness, behavior, deportment in public, or a parent's manner of speech, way of asking questions, or areas of concern, and come to conclusions about family life, the quality of parenting, and a child's abilities at school.

Ideas about being a "good parent" can function as a "script" for parents (Lopez, 2001, p. 417). The good parent outlines the preferred way to engage with schools if they want their children's needs to be acknowledged. However, the good parent image is not universal. It assumes that all parents share values, hopes, and dreams, and importantly, it assumes that the problems families face are uniform. (Lopez, 2001). In fact, families have different beliefs about their children's education and families have a range of experiences within schools. Unfortunately, when parents have a significant disagreement or problem with any part of their child's school experience, there is no clear path for engaging in deep conversation across substantial differences. The ideal of the "good parent" does not include advocacy or conflict.

Ideas about what it means to be a "good" parent vary from region to region, from one social identity to another, and from culture to culture (LeVine and LeVine, 2017). However, in the United States, the dominant view of good parenting prioritizes stereotypical middle- and upper-class parenting preferences. Lareau et al. (2018) observe that school districts in high-income communities are typically comprised of families with both plenty of disposable income and "abundant" noneconomic resources (p. 1). The success of these districts, Lareau et al. assert, is "highly symbolic" (p. 2). The schools and the families, who attend them, serve as a pinnacle, a benchmark, against which all public schools are measured, regardless of their resources. If ideas about "good parenting" are left unchecked, they can have a negative impact on the family-school relationship because they shroud important differences among families.

The family-school relationship

Over the past five decades, ideas about the family-school relationship and how best to engage families have evolved. In the 1980s and 1990s, involving families was seen as an activity-based endeavor. Education was considered a shared responsibility within which educators designated "educational responsibilities" for families to implement at home (Epstein 2011; Rich, 1987, pp. 26–28). Parents typically played a passive role in this relationship, simply implementing the school's vision. For example, interactive homework required parents to work with their children on specific assignments (Van Voorhis, 2011). The parent literacy program in my school is a perfect example of activity-based family involvement. Certainly, programs like this have benefits, but without relationships and understanding of a family's social awareness, they can also cause complications.

Relational engagement

Activity-based parent involvement soon yielded to the importance of relationships in education, because school is an "intrinsically social enterprise" (Bryk and Schneider, 2004, p. 19). Ignoring the family-school relationships, as I did with Joe and Gail, can create or exacerbate, rather than resolve problems. Educational researcher Soo Hong (2011) asserts that:

> Parent engagement is not a fixed set of activities but a dynamic, evolving, and context-specific process that requires us to break with tradition and consider

> multiple perspectives, varied experiences and the myriad dimensions of culture and power. (p. 188)

By the 2000s, building effective relationships with families became the cornerstone and educators strived for the "meaningful involvement of parents" (p. 271). Meaningful engagement includes a sharing of power between the school and families, and the creation of a culture in which family concerns are taken seriously and treated with respect. Further research reinforces these ideas (Bryk and Schneider, 2004; Comer and Haynes, 1991; Francis et al., 2016; Geller, 2016; Ishimaru et al., 2015), with one study noting that "the importance of these relationships cannot be stressed enough" (Underwood and Killoran, 2012, p. 393).

The evolution of parent engagement from "activity-focused" to "relationship-building" is evident in the language used to describe it. And so, what started as "parent involvement" became "family engagement"—a difference which emphasizes the broad variety of families in schools and importance of the give-and-take of engagement. Larry Ferlazzo (2011) defines "parent involvement" as "lead[ing] with their *mouths*"—in other words, telling parents what to do. On the other hand, he defines "family engagement" as "lead[ing] with their *ears*" (p. 10)"—prioritizing listening to families. This is a difference which allows educators to attend to the many social factors which influence a family's relationship with a school and to consider the "complex ways that interact with family background and social context variables" (Baker and Soden, 1998, p. 3). While the family-school relationship has potential for positive educational outcomes for students (Epstein, 2011; Mapp and Kuttner, 2013), the benefits of these practices vary depending on social identities such as race, ethnicity, and socioeconomic status (Hill and Taylor, 2004; Robinson and Harris, 2014).

I'd like to pause here and note a crucial missing element. These mainstream tenets of the family-school relationship do not include parent as *advocate*, nor do they account for *conflict*. The education of children touches the most basic values of both parents and teachers. Both parties are heavily invested in creating a positive school experience and setting children on the path to a successful future. This is important work on the parts of both parents and teachers. Advocacy and conflict are natural outcomes of conversations around the most important parts of life. Educators only need tools to successfully navigate these parts of the family-school relationship.

The educator and parent advocacy

The focus of this book, advocacy, is the point at which the values and visions of a family meet the expertise and experience of school staff. Since social identities provide different social and educational contexts, a one-size-fits-all approach to working with families will exclude some. Educators can learn to recognize and work with parent advocacy across social identities.

Social identity impacts the family-school relationship and informs parent advocacy. For that reason, educators must "confront them head-on" (Hong, 2011, p. 196). Without a deliberate consideration of these issues, we risk falling back into an idealized view of the family-school connection and expecting all families to embody the "good parent." For example, sometimes educators expect families to be passive (Baquedano-Lopez, Alexander, and Hernandez, 2013; Warren and Mapp, 2011). School employees with this view may expect families to be polite and deferential and, because of that, some parent feedback may be seen as unreasonable, rather than being evaluated on its merits (Cooper, 2009; Lareau and Horvat, 1999; Lareau and Muñoz, 2012). This expectation makes it difficult for families to present areas of disagreement to educators and have their concerns taken seriously.

However, educators can mitigate these concerns by developing awareness of the ways social identities such as religion, family structure, home language, immigration status, special education students, and more influence both the family-school relationship and parent advocacy. As American schools become increasingly diverse, educators use family social identities to build a deeper family-school relationship and meet the needs of all students.

Discussion questions

- What are your social identities? Reflect on your social identities and how they may have influenced your life.
- How do you define "good parenting"? Outline your definition of "good parenting" and the "why" behind your views. In groups, discuss:
  - Where do our ideas come from?
  - What experiences in life led us to this definition?
  - How are our definitions similar to/different from others?
- What is parent advocacy? Have you ever experienced this (as a child, as a parent, as a teacher)? In groups, discuss:
  - What happened?
  - How did this advocacy make you feel?

- o Was this parent advocacy successful? That is, did it achieve the desired goal?

Extension activities

- "Every student has the right to learn in a safe and accepting school environment" (Orr and Baum, p. 3). What does this statement mean to you? Have you felt unsafe in your career in school? Have you known others who have felt unsafe? Choose an example or use the story of Ada's daughter to create a one-paragraph personal philosophy on creating a safe and accepting school environment.
- Reflect on families you've encountered in your life—as a student, a teacher, or in other capacities. What parental concerns have you observed? List them. How did families work to address their concerns?

1
Race and ethnicity
"Oh, he's just a troublemaker."

Chapter learning objectives
Gain new perspective by discovering how systemic biases regarding race and ethnicity influence the family-school relationship and shift the way parents advocate for their students of color.

Introduction
Racial and ethnic identities of students and their families impact the way teachers and other school staff see children and understand their successes and struggles. Likewise, families respond to racially and ethnically biased misunderstandings of their students through engagement with the school and advocacy for their child. This chapter illustrates three types of bias which impact Emily and her 8-year-old son, Lewis, and Angela and her 16-year-old son, Adan. Emily's and Angela's experiences illuminate the power of implicit racial and ethnic biases on students and families, the advocacy needed to address them, and how teachers can mitigate the negative impact of preconceptions in their teaching practice.

Vignettes

These vignettes are adapted from Lee, 2020. Names and identifying features have been changed.

Emily and Lewis's story

Emily and her children lived in an affluent town, more than 90 percent white with a median income of approximately $150,000 per year. This figure was more than double the state's median income. Emily's own income—less than $40,000 per year—made her an outlier. Located outside a large city in the northeast of the United States, this community of about 40,000 residents was home to six elementary schools, two middle schools, and one high school. Emily's youngest, Lewis, attended their local elementary school, which was both whiter and more affluent than the other schools in town. As a single, white mother living in affordable housing with three Black children, Emily's family were outliers on many fronts. Lewis, in grade 3, was not thriving. Academically, he struggled to stay on task. His energy fully expended at school, he would arrive home and collapse from sadness and exhaustion. He hated school.

Emily approached the school with the idea of testing her son for Attention Deficit and Hyperactivity Disorder (ADHD). However, while the teacher and special education coordinator acknowledged that her son was struggling, they dismissed her concerns with "Oh, he's just a troublemaker." This was not the first time she'd heard this view from school employees. One day she picked her sons up from the after-hours program at their school. Looking for her children, she found them, not in their activities, but sitting in the office with the head of the after-school program.

Emily shared that "she had a very stern look on her face. I asked, 'Why are they here?' 'They're **always** causing trouble.'" Probing, Emily got the full story. Lewis had been talking in chess class, breaking the "silent rule" the chess teacher had imposed on her first through third graders.

While both family and school acknowledged a problem, they disagreed about the root cause and therefore they disagreed about how to address it. Emily saw indications of ADHD while the school saw a discipline issue. According to Emily, the educators rejected the possibility of ADHD, "just insisting that he was being stubborn and difficult." Unable to change minds and faced with a disciplinary approach to what she believed was a common problem for many students, she pulled her son out of school and enrolled him in the state's online accredited public school. She researched and engaged free and low-cost community supports. In a matter of months, Lewis was diagnosed with ADHD and began receiving support.

Eventually, Emily returned to the school, this time accompanied by her son's team. And this time, the teacher and special education liaison listened. They accepted that Lewis's behavior was caused by his ADHD rather than by deliberate, defiant behavior and created an Individualized Education Program (IEP) to support him. The entire process took more than six months. Emily summed up her experience this way: "If I were a different parent, with a white child, from a wealthy family with two parents—it [taking Lewis out of school] never would have happened."

Angela and Adan's story

Angela, single mom to a struggling high school student, shared a similar experience. She and her children identified as Latinx, were bilingual, and lived in subsidized housing in a primarily white and high-income community of around 30,000 residents. The oldest of four, Adan began struggling with mental health issues at the beginning of high school. His mother supported treatment for depression, coordinated with his high school by providing information, tracking Adan's progress, and working with the high school to support him. One day, Adan and his friends were caught smoking in the high school bathroom. Although not "the leader" of this misadventure, Adan received an out-of-school suspension. His two white counterparts received in-school suspensions. When he returned, Adan ate lunch in the office while his friends ate in the cafeteria.

Adan was embarrassed to be singled out for meriting more significant punishment. Angela, also perplexed by this discrepancy, reached out to the school to ask why her son's punishment was different from that of his friends. Angela was unsettled and confused about why school administrators would opt for punishment instead of support, given Adan's fragile mental health. She requested a meeting at which she posed this question. In response, school leaders told her she was overly sensitive and being "defensive." So Angela requested another meeting, at which she shared her feelings plainly, asking, "Is it because they're white and my son's a little bit darker?" The educators said "no" and declared the conversation closed. Angela concluded that not only were these staff members unable to support her son in the ways he required, but they were also unable to understand the broader and deeper role race and ethnicity were playing in her son's education. The next day she moved Adan to a different high school.

Emily, Angela, and their children experienced biased and therefore unproductive interactions with teachers, specialists, and administrators. In both cases, these experiences resulted in substantial disruptions to student learning and family life. When Emily commented that "it" would never have had happened if she had a different profile, she connected it—the negative views of Lewis to implicit biases held by school personnel about Black children. Likewise, Angela drew a straight line between school staff biases around race to unfair treatment of her son.

The vignettes above illustrate common ways in which families, whose racial and ethnic identities are Black and Hispanic, experience bias in their interactions with schools, and convey the impact of bias on student and family well-being. This chapter focuses on three concerns: deficit views of racially and ethnically diverse students and their families, narrow expectations of family advocacy, and the discipline gap. These concerns emerge from implicit biases on the part of school personnel and directly influence a family's ability to interact with school staff and to advocate for their children. In essence, these factors create a bind for families, forcing them to choose between advocating for their children in an "acceptable" manner, which often is ignored and dismissed, or engaging in more assertive advocacy which draws attention to their child's needs, but paints them in an unfavorable light.

Vocabulary

In this chapter, I use the phrases *racial identities* and *ethnic identities* in alignment with the definitions of the US Census Bureau. The Census Bureau states that "the racial categories included in the census questionnaire generally reflect a social definition of race recognized in this country and not an attempt to define race biologically, anthropologically, or genetically" (US Census Bureau, 2022).

> **American Indian or Alaska Native:** "A person having origins in any of the original peoples of North and South America (including Central America) and who maintains tribal affiliation or community attachment."
>
> **Asian:** "A person having origins in any of the original peoples of the Far East, Southeast Asia, or the Indian subcontinent including, for example, Cambodia, China, India, Japan, Korea, Malaysia, Pakistan, the Philippine Islands, Thailand, and Vietnam."
>
> **Black or African American:** "A person having origins in any of the Black racial groups of Africa."
>
> **Native Hawaiian or Other Pacific Islander:** "A person having origins in any of the original peoples of Hawaii, Guam, Samoa, or other Pacific Islands."
>
> **White:** "A person having origins in any of the original peoples of Europe, the Middle East, or North Africa."
>
> **Two or More Races:** Bi- and multi-racial residents of the United States.
>
> (US Census Bureau, 2022)

Ethnicity, according to the US Census Bureau (2021), is separate from race. "Each person has two attributes, their race (or races) and whether or not they are Hispanic." The US Census Bureau highlights an important aspect of racial and ethnic categorizations. Race is a socially created idea based on superficial characteristics such as appearance or country of one's ancestors.

"Implicit bias" describes unconscious assumptions which lead to favoritism of some groups and prejudice against other groups. Everyone carries implicit biases with them which influence their day-to-day interactions.

Reflection

Before we explore these vignettes more closely, take a moment to reflect on your initial reactions to the stories of Emily, Angela, and their children. Using the shared definitions above, answer the following questions:

1. What similarities and/or differences do you see between Emily's and Angela's stories?
2. How might implicit biases have influenced the way school staff viewed, and worked with, Lewis and Adan?
3. How might implicit biases have influenced the relationship between each parent and their child's team in these examples?

Deficit views and parent advocacy

Both Emily's and Angela's stories illustrate how deficit views, based on students' racial and/or ethnic identities, play critical roles in the ways school employees relate to families. First, deficit views can include negative assumptions about the potential of students and also about how their parents interact with the school. Deficit views "emphasize what [parents and students] lack instead of stressing what they contribute" (Cooper, 2009, p. 382). Negative preconceptions exist about many marginalized groups. However, in general, educators are more likely to see students and families who are Black or Hispanic in a negative light, mirroring common racial stereotypes in broader society (Gandara and Contreras, 2009; Marchand et al., 2019; Rothstein, 2004; Shapiro, 2004). For example, Black parents are simultaneously seen as "uninvolved" (Marchand et al., p. 367) and "intimidating, confrontational, and uninformed" (Love et al., 2021, p. 640).

Deficit views do more than complicate relationships between students and teachers. They also delegitimize parenting approaches which diverge from the school's preferences. For example, Torres and Hurtado-Vivas (2011) describe a literacy engagement program at the elementary level which ignored existing Latinx family literacy activities, such as reading the Bible, and prioritized school activities because they did not match the school's view. Instead, school staff required families to enact school literacy programming which exemplified "acceptable" involvement. Here, a deficit view of culturally relevant literacy practices missed an opportunity to work within existing literacy practices.

Lewis's teachers viewed his actions from a deficit position when they assumed that he was being purposefully inappropriate and disruptive. This assumption reflects a common bias in society— the idea that Black boys are out of control, deliberately bad, and dangerous. Moreover, Lewis's teachers departed from basic teaching. Rather than analyzing how and when Lewis struggled and anchoring their views in observation and child development, they focused on the outward manifestations of Lewis's struggles. They mistook the outward signs of a problem for the problem itself.

Deficit views—are you a gatekeeper or an ally?

Gatekeeper	Ally
Refused to consider the possibility of ADHD (or other possible diagnoses) as the underlying reason for Lewis's behavior.	Balances student strengths alongside challenges and separates surface behaviors from underlying issues. Teachers look to address both the immediate problems and the root causes.
Were unwilling to consider whether implicit racial biases could influence their conclusions.	Recognizes that we all have implicit biases and actively considers in each circumstance whether biases are at play and in which areas.
Ignored deficit views of Lewis and Adan and were content to believe that their struggles were primarily behavioral.	Actively manages their own responses to racism and integrate anti-racist and culturally responsive teaching into their teaching by recognizing embedded racist practices, working to remove them, and remaining open to the myriad of contextual factors influencing schooling.

Deepen your practice

How can teachers reposition their view of classroom problems? Ask whether a student's issues are centered solely on the child and family. Brainstorm ways in which the school environment might be influencing or exacerbating circumstances.

Flip the script by considering the issues from other perspectives

Focus on a student in your current class or placement or use one of the examples above. Write out the primary concern you/your school has about this student. Brainstorm various ways other stakeholders might see their behavior. What might their mother say? Their therapist?

"Acceptable" parent advocacy

Parent involvement with schools is frequently defined as coming into schools and offering "deferential" and unquestioning support for school programs and goals. Likewise, "acceptable" advocacy is guided by the idea that parents will be compliant and supportive of school goals. These expectations serve as a laundry list—that defines what "good parents" should do (Marchand et al., 2019, p. 372). In fact, these ideas are so widespread that they are rendered nearly invisible. Expectations of "acceptable" interactions form a script, a map which parents are expected to follow. When parents depart from that script, school personnel perceive them as violating the rules. From the perspective of school personnel, this is unexpected, unwelcome, and interpreted as poor parenting. Prioritizing deferential support requires parents to trust the school even around hard topics like race and racism, a trust which is often not earned. However, remaining within the boundaries of "acceptable advocacy" may allow real harm to continue to both students and their parents.

In the United States, traditional expectations of parental involvement and advocacy emerge from and are rooted in "privilege[d], white, middle-class, behavior norms" (Cooper, 2009, p. 381). The example by Torres and Hurtado-Vivas (2011) illustrates how schools might unwittingly give precedence to their point of view. Educators assumed that a school-developed literacy program was superior to current family literacy practices. Their approach was "best," while a culturally specific form was overlooked. Parent advocacy encompasses a much wider range of circumstances than is acceptable through traditional pathways.

Research indicates that parents of Black and Hispanic students act as "agents of change" in their student's school (Marchand et al., 2019, p. 368) and focus not only on their child's learning, but also on the broader atmosphere of the school. Such advocacy is motivated by a parent's understanding of the impact systemic inequities in the school setting have on children (Love et al., 2021). This type of advocacy strives to make issues within the school setting visible and to highlight the impact of "achievement gaps," "racialized student tracking," "inequitable school funding," and different rates of disciplining, among others, on children of color (Marchand et al., 2019, p. 369).

Under these circumstances, parents of Black and Hispanic students do not have the luxury of simply focusing on their child's education. They must simultaneously support their child academically while also working to mitigate the impact of a racist system on their child. As Love et al. (2021) state, they must "strategically resist marginalization" (p. 638). Thus, advocacy can appear to be "defensive" (Marchand et al., 2019, p. 374) because it violates the unspoken assumptions defining parent advocacy. In short, by adhering to a narrow definition of advocacy, teachers and administrators risk misinterpreting the advocacy necessary to address substantial and entrenched inequities in their classrooms.

"The Value of Hard Work" Lopez (2001) offers another example of unrecognized advocacy. In the Padilla family, the parents were migrant workers, and they required both of their children to participate in migrant field work. Their focus was not to generate income. Instead, they wanted their children to gain a first-hand understanding that field work was hard, and the compensation was inadequate. Doing so underscored the power of education to open other, and better, opportunities. Mr Padilla stated, "You have doors in front of you, son" (p. 432). Faced with a powerful example of the power of education, both children excelled at school and continued to college and careers. However, this powerful parent advocacy would not be recognized as such by schools.

Both Emily and Angela asserted that their unsuccessful interactions with schools emerged from underlying assumptions about their child based on skin color and advocated for the support their sons needed. Emily recognized that the school's view of her son matched society's deficit views of Black boys. When her advocacy included this point, she departed from the script of acceptable advocacy and defied the expectation of deference and unquestioning support.

Likewise, Angela's advocacy for Adan challenged the expectation of parental deference. Rather than considering whether her son's punishment was, in fact, harsher than that of his friends, they labeled Angela's anger as defensiveness—another common stereotype. In expressing her anger, Angela attempted to highlight the role that race played in Adan's everyday experience in school; however, her advocacy departed from the acceptable. This left Angela, and Adan, with limited options.

Acceptable advocacy—are you a gatekeeper or an ally?

Gatekeeper	Ally
Expects deference from parents and negates their contributions if they do not express ideas in the acceptable way.	Understands and is prepared for a variety of parent responses during difficult conversations.
Listens and asks clarifying questions.	Will not admit to mistakes or explore their personal role in challenging parent encounters.
Commits to being uncomfortable, making mistakes, apologizing, and asking for help when needed.	

Deepen your practice

How can teachers recognize parent advocacy? Consider your own expectations. Brainstorm what you think parent advocacy "should" look like. Review your list—do you think these approaches will be effective for every parent? Add potential difficulties families might face with each expectation you've listed. After reading this section, can you describe any parent actions which you did not see as advocacy—but do now?

How might you advocate for all families in your classroom? List ways you could share the needs of your families with other teachers and administrators. What do you think they need to know about how families advocate for their children? Choose one idea and describe it to a peer.

Advocating across the discipline gap

Angela advocated for Adan by questioning why his punishments were harsher than those of his white friends. Adan's stricter consequences illustrate the "discipline gap" among students of different racial and ethnic identities. The phrase "discipline gap" refers to documented differences in the type and severity of punishments among students of different races and ethnicities (Young, Young, and Butler, 2018). Research confirms and reconfirms that not only does a gap exists, but it also exists at every level across the K-12 continuum.

For example, research demonstrates that Black students are "more than twice as likely to incur school discipline actions" than their white counterparts (Young, Young, and Butler, 2018,

p. 106). Moreover, Black students receive more "suspensions and expulsions," while white students receive "minor office referrals." Black students are also more likely than their white peers to be expelled from school. Overall, "the odds of being disciplined if Black are more than two and half times the odds of being disciplined if white" (p. 95).

The impact of the discipline gap is significant. First, it disrupts the education of students of color. Black and Hispanic students are pulled out of class for disciplinary reasons or suspended from school more frequently and for longer periods and therefore they miss more class time than their peers. This gap has also been implicated in the "school-to-prison pipeline" (Young, Young, and Butler, 2018, p. 96).

Constant harsh discipline also results in emotional challenges. In Adan's case, his education was disrupted multiple times and at higher rates than his white peers. Not only did he receive suspension, but his mother also removed him from that school and enrolled him in another school.

The discipline gap—are you a gatekeeper or an ally?

Gatekeeper	Ally
Sees punishment for poor behavior as the primary path to ameliorating problems.	Pivots from discipline to support and recognizes that a student receiving appropriate supports is less likely to act out (Love et al., 2021).

Gatekeeper	Ally
Will not admit to mistakes or explore their personal role in challenging parent encounters.	Commits to being uncomfortable, making mistakes, apologizing, and asking for help when needed.

Deepen your practice

Is there a discipline gap in your classroom or school? How could you find out? Consider tracking disciplinary practices in your own classroom over the course of a month. Reflect on what you see and generate ways to improve.

The parent advocacy bind

The intersection of deficit views of students and families and narrow ideas about "acceptable advocacy" binds parents with Black and Brown racial and ethnic identities into an impossible situation (Love et al., 2021). Parents are expected to work with school communities which are unreceptive, judgmental, and dismissive of their advocacy, even when it occurs in "acceptable" forms. At the same time, parents like Emily and Angela are grappling with substantial and damaging concerns about discrimination. Some, like Lewis, are struggling on many levels, not only academically but also physically and emotionally. Parents in this bind face a "paradox" (Love et al., 2021, p. 639). Teacher biases create an unfriendly atmosphere for Black students and parents. They must navigate an environment in which "they are pathologized if they do interact with schools and vilified if they do not" (Marchand et al., 2019, p. 374). For example,

Black families are expected to participate in a deferential manner while weighted down by common stereotypes that they are "disconnected, aggressive and confrontational" (Cooper, 2009, p. 381).

Emily's and Angela's input not only violated acceptable advocacy, but they were also not seen as useful or informed. Emily and Angela were dismissed because, in the eyes of the school, they lacked the authority to participate as equals in discussions regarding their own child's education. They, their questions, and their concerns were dismissed.

Unconventional advocacy (Marchand, 2019, p. 376)

In both vignettes, Emily's and Angela's advocacy was initially dismissed, even though they employed acceptable scripts, requested meetings, asked questions, and asked for support. Both parents pushed back against the perspectives offered by school staff, and both introduced the possibility of racial or ethnic biases on the part of school staff. Their perspectives were rejected, and Emily and Angela left frustrated by the educators' refusal to engage on topics deeply important to them and central to their child's future. Traditional advocacy routes were unsuccessful; however, the issues facing their sons were intolerable. Emily and Angela found themselves in the bind that forced their advocacy off-script.

Bold gestures

It was only after Emily unenrolled her son, gathered her own information, and brought her son's team to meet with the school, that school leaders considered, and eventually agreed with, her concerns. Likewise, Angela pulled Adan from that school setting and immediately enrolled him in a neighboring school. Dismissal of parent advocacy requires parents to regroup and find alternative ways to protect and support their children. First, and perhaps most importantly, both mothers immediately took resolute action. They removed their sons from an unjust, discriminatory, and toxic setting. Second, taking bold action served to underscore foundational importance of their complaints. Through action, both parents told their schools that their lack of acceptable response and their unwillingness to protect children was so egregious that they no longer trusted the school with their children.

Cautious anger

Additionally, Angela used anger judiciously to draw attention to an injustice. She sums up her predicament clearly: "When I'm nice, I kinda feel like I get brushed off a bit. So, I'm like no, let's not be nice this time" (Lee, 2020, p. 128). Anger emphasized Angela's concerns after they had been downplayed. And anger has the potential to jumpstart a conversation and move all parties toward resolution. Unfortunately, anger can also play into and reinforce deficit views of parents. In Angela's situation, educators saw her as "defensive." They used that label to minimize and dismiss her concerns about discrimination.

Parents in this bind have a choice to make. Do they continue to advocate through traditional and acceptable practices, even if that is not likely to resolve the issues impacting their child? Or do they break out of acceptable advocacy and highlight the significance and the impact of the problem, even if they will be labeled as defensive, angry, or indifferent? When parents pursue unconventional paths to advocacy, schools can dismiss their concerns through the deficit stereotypes described earlier. The discomfort of these circumstances is attributed to parent behavior and not to the climate of the school.

The parent bind– are you a gatekeeper or an ally?

Gatekeeper	Ally
Does not look beyond the superficial when interacting with students and families.	Listens and takes notes. Asks questions about points they don't understand. Looks beyond the presentation.
Does not recognize or appreciate the parent bind.	Works to avoid putting parents in a bind.

Deepen your practice

- How might you discover invisible engagement and advocacy? Make visible the bind parents find themselves in. Advocate in your school for a broader definition of advocacy.
- Instead of dismissing parents as uninvolved, defensive, or unresponsive, ask "What prompted the response I'm seeing? What might lead a parent to respond in this way?"

Chapter discussion questions

- Why do you think this chapter is titled "Oh he's just a troublemaker"?

- Why is it important for teachers to remain aware of deficit views in their teaching?
- How did your family of origin see and understand race? When did your family first talk to you about race? Do you agree with your family's or community's beliefs about racial and ethnic identities? Have your views changed? Why and how?
- How has your racial identity impacted your life? How has it impacted your schooling? Your teaching?
- In small groups, brainstorm diverse ways to engage with families. Share, discuss. Which one(s) can you implement easily? Which might be challenging?

Extension activities

- Develop a survey for families. How will you assess the priorities of your family population?
- Flip through a magazine or school-related website—pay attention to the ads.
  - Who do you see in ads?
  - Who don't you see in ads?
  - What patterns emerge?
  - If you had no other information about schooling in your area, what assumptions would you take away from this resource?

  Case studies—You are a teacher and…
o All the Black and Brown students are in your classroom in a primarily white setting. Parents of these students are questioning how this segregation occurred. What can you do?

o   You are incorporating discussions of inclusion and exclusion into your middle school social studies curriculum. After discussing common stereotypes that Black and Hispanic students face in schools, a group of parents, with students who identify as Asian, approach you and ask why the unit did not include discrimination against Asians. How do you respond? What stereotypes might these students and their families face at school?

2
Ability

"No one else gets how hard it is."

Chapter learning objectives

Gain understanding of the obstacles families with children with needs face and learn how this impacts the family-school relationships and parent advocacy.

Introduction

Across the globe, more than 240 million children have been diagnosed with educational needs which require special approaches to education. This amounts to roughly one in every ten children, worldwide, requiring education which specifically meets their needs; unsurprisingly, these children "face multiple and compounding challenges in realizing their rights" (UNICEF, 2021). In the United States alone, approximately 7.2 million children are identified as having a disability and received services in the 2020–2021 school years (NCES, 2022). Parents work hard to ensure that their students receive an excellent education in general and with regard to their specific needs. Moreover, in many countries such as the United States, schools are required to involve parents in the process of creating educational plans. This approach encourages parents to advocate for their students.

The term "special education" refers to specially designed instruction that includes services or programs focused to meet a child's particular need (National PTA). Special education encompasses a broad and diverse range of conditions including students with physical impairments such as blindness, intellectual disabilities like Down syndrome, learning challenges, and emotional disturbances, among others. As mentioned in Chapter 1, in the United States, the most common diagnosis receiving support is "specific learning disability" (NCES, 2022). This category accounts for approximately 33 percent of students receiving special education in the United States (NCES, 2022). In many countries, including the United States, schools are mandated to provide education to all children regardless of need. Although different categories of special education may require different forms of advocacy and intervention, families with special needs children share common barriers to, and problems with, advocacy.

In this chapter, we use "person-first" language as described in the introduction. It is important to acknowledge that, given the range of abilities described above, not every group agrees that person-first language is appropriate. For example, not all families with members on the autism spectrum use this approach. For many, autism is not a disability, but part of the typical variation in humans (Loftus, 2021). In this scenario, person-first language emphasizes a typical trait and, by highlighting it, implies a deficit where none exists. Since this chapter does look broadly at disabilities, we will continue to use a person-first approach.

Vignettes

Eve and Toby's story

Eve lives in the suburb of a mid-sized midwestern city with her husband and their two boys, Toby, age ten and Timothy, age eight. Their community of 45,000 is predominantly white, with a median household income over 30 percent higher than that of the state. Eve knew from early on that both her children were different from their peers. However, for Toby, his struggles came to a head at the beginning of third grade. Before the school year started, Eve reached out to Toby's teacher, Ms Shah, described her son and "offered to help her navigate any challenges." Through the beginning of the year, Ms Shah noted that Toby was unable to follow the flow of classroom routines. When asked to change activities or transition into another subject or location, he would either shut down—for example, crawling under a desk and refusing to come out—or melt down with disruptive behavior, which required the teacher's full attention to address.

Ms Shah called Eve for information, a choice which Eve sees as the pivot point for Toby's school experience. Eve stated that she understood how much time it took to meet Toby's needs and it was clear that "she really cared about him." Eve noted, "Here was a kid in grade 3, struggling to simply get through the day. Instead of being like 'oh god, I have this behavior problem in my class', she called me and asked questions about how to help him." Together, Ms Shah and Eve figured out that Toby would need a quiet place to read, a walk through the hallway, or time in the sensory room, a space designed for students with sensory processing challenges. Moreover, Ms

Shah realized that she couldn't manage these interventions as the sole teacher in the classroom. She needed a co-teacher or an aide and began to advocate for Toby at the school and district level.

Looking back, Eve recognizes that Ms Shah was an outstanding teacher. She was proactive in supporting Toby even though he did not yet have a diagnosis or an IEP. Thanks to Ms Shah's advocacy and school resources, she received an aide dedicated to Toby. Their primary role was to help Toby manage his school day, leaving the teacher free to manage the classroom. Ms Shah was able to create a positive school environment, not only for Toby, but also for rest of the class. Eve reflected that "an excellent teacher can make all the difference," and she credits Ms Shah with successfully bridging the gap between Toby's initial struggles and his formal diagnosis of autism, and his official IEP—approximately five months later.

Emily and Lewis's story

The next vignette revisits Emily and Lewis's story from Chapter 1. Their experiences in the public schools encompass three common social identifiers: race, ability, and socioeconomic status. In this chapter, we will examine their story through the lens of ability. Emily and her children lived in an affluent town, more than 90 percent white with a median income of approximately $150,000 per year. This figure was more than double the state's median income. Emily's own income (less than $40,000 per year) made her an outlier. Located outside a large city in the northeast of the United States, this community of about 40,000 residents was home to six elementary schools, two middle schools and one high school. Her youngest, Lewis, attended their local elementary school which was both whiter and more affluent than the other schools in town. As a single, white mother, living in affordable housing with three Black children, Emily's family were outliers on many fronts. Lewis, in grade 3, was not thriving. Academically, he struggled to stay on task. His energy fully expended at school, he would arrive home and collapse from sadness and exhaustion. He hated school.

Emily approached the school with the idea of testing her son for ADHD. However, while the teacher and special education coordinator acknowledged that her son was struggling, they dismissed her concerns with, "Oh, he's just a troublemaker." This was not the first time she'd heard this view from school employees. One day she picked her sons up from the after-hours program at their school. Looking for her children, she found them, not in their activities, but sitting in the office with the head of the after-school program. Emily shared that "she had a very stern look on her face. I asked, 'Why are they here?' 'They're **always** causing trouble.'" Probing, Emily got the full story. Lewis had been talking in chess class, breaking the "silent rule" the chess teacher had imposed on her first through third graders.

While both family and school acknowledged a problem, they disagreed about the root cause and, therefore, they disagreed about how to address it. Emily saw indications of ADHD while the school saw a discipline issue. According to Emily, the educators rejected the possibility of ADHD, "just insisting that he was being stubborn and difficult." Unable to change minds and faced with a disciplinary approach to what she believed was a common problem for many students, she pulled her son out of school and enrolled him in the state's online accredited public school. She researched and engaged free and low-cost community supports. In a matter of months, Lewis was diagnosed with ADHD and began receiving support.

Eventually, Emily returned to the school, this time accompanied by her son's team. And this time, the teacher and special education liaison listened. They accepted that Lewis's behavior was caused by his ADHD rather than by deliberate, defiant behavior and created an IEP to support him. The entire process took more than six months. Emily summed up her experience this way: "If I were a different parent, with a white child, from a wealthy family with two parents—it (teachers focusing on Lewis's behavior rather than his academic needs) never would have happened."

Cassie and Joseph's story

Cassie first realized that her son needed extra support at Back-to-School Night in fifth grade. Their local school was small, creating a comfortable and intimate community. Like the other elementary schools in her midwestern suburban community of approximately 50,000 people, Joseph's school was nearly 90 percent white and over 90 percent high income. Their town's median household income was 2.5 times higher than the state average. As she wandered the classroom and looked at classwork on display, she realized that Joseph's schoolwork looked very different from that of his peers. It was obviously less mature, messier, and incomplete. Moreover, when the parents were asked to sit in their child's seat for the presentation, she discovered that Joseph was separated from his peers. The rest of the class was clustered in groups of four and five, but Joseph's desk was isolated, positioned by the teacher's desk at the front and center of the room. Even as an adult, sitting in the center of a fishbowl felt embarrassing. Not only had she not known there were issues in the classroom, she, and every other parent in attendance, had just found out—simply by the placement of his desk.

The next day, Cassie contacted the teacher, Mrs Jordan, to hear more about Joseph's school experience, but right away the meeting became contentious. From the outset, Cassie noted that Mrs Jordan "didn't give off a vibe of partnership." For example, when Cassie asked whether her son's schoolwork was at grade level, the teacher commented, "Well yes, he doesn't write like a normal person" and "He's a bit of an oddball." Although Cassie was taken aback by Mrs Jordan's description, she assumed that they were in agreement regarding her son's need for extra support. However, as Cassie began to ask about appropriate interventions and school supports, she was surprised that Mrs Jordan adamantly disagreed. According to her, Joseph's struggles did not meet the threshold of extra support. For the next five months, Cassie continued the conversation to no avail. Her son continued to struggle and began to dislike school, so Cassie requested her son be officially evaluated. The school declined.

At this turning point, Cassie began to actively advocate for Joseph. First, she had him assessed privately, a process which gave a name to his challenges. This information relieved Cassie. Not only did she have an explanation for Joseph's struggles, but she was also able to find concrete resources to support him. Then, she consulted with a lawyer who advised her to write a letter to the district and helped her use phrases which directly connected to language in IEPs, thereby building her case. Moreover, Cassie stated "it was not a friendly letter." Only then did her son's school evaluate him, create an IEP, and begin to use interventions in the classroom. This experience was deeply stressful, and Cassie noted that her success in meeting her son's needs was only possible because her family had resources. Like Eve, the median household income of Cassie's community was more than twice that of the state. She and her husband were able to pay for private testing, pay to consult an attorney, and Cassie put her skills as a professional writer and communicator to work. Reflecting on her experience, she notes that "to have a choice changes everything" and money increases a family's options. "The system is broken. I want to belong to a different system."

Common vocabulary

Ableism—"the systematic oppression of peoples with (perceived) disabilities. Ableism is based on the assumption that there is a physical, intellectual, and emotional standard for human beings and that this standard is the only one accepted as normal" (Sensoy and Diangelo, 2017, p. 221).

Special Education (SPED)—is grounded in the idea that every child, no matter their abilities, should have access to education. Special education refers to the systems in place to provide appropriate services to meet students' needs.

Individualized Education Program (IEP)—is a written plan required by law that documents how the school staff will meet the needs of a particular student.

Reflection

- For each vignette, list the ways their child's teacher supported or could have supported them.
- How comfortable did each parent feel advocating for their child?
- What barriers existed for each family which prevented them from advocating for their child?
- What surprised you about each parent's experience advocating for their child?

In this chapter, we examine three challenges parents face when navigating the special education system in their child's school: (1) gaining knowledge about their child's needs and about their child's rights under the law; (2) the emotional impact of caring for, educating, and advocating for a child with needs; and (3) the impact of family and school resources on a parent's ability to advocate.

Knowledgeable advocacy

Faced with a special education diagnosis for their child, parents commonly lack knowledge in two critical areas (Luelmo and Kasari, 2021). While authors Luelmo and Kasari focus specifically on Latinx parents of children with autism, these two areas are universally important. First, parents need to learn about their child's diagnosis. Often, parents are starting this journey at a very basic level. They wonder and worry—what will their child need to be successful at school? What barriers exist for them? Which educational interventions will produce the best results, and will their child's school agree to implement them? Above all, how can they work alongside the school to create the best possible future for their child?

Gaining knowledge about their child's needs is its own challenge. Parents must decode medical terminology and educational jargon, while also digesting information about how to support their child (Buren, Rios, and Burke, 2021). This is a lengthy process, and it takes time for a parent to develop the background they need to participate in the special education process. Even for parents with familiarity with a diagnosis, "you don't know what you don't know," which creates a dilemma because sometimes parents don't know "what to ask for" (p. 15). Parents bring critical knowledge about their children; when you couple this with deep understanding of their needs and rights, parent advocacy is best situated to benefit the child.

Parents also face a lack of knowledge about the complex laws which govern students with needs. In the United States, these laws fall under the Individuals with Disabilities Education Act (IDEA). Among IDEA's many provisions is the expectation that students must be educated in the least restrictive environment, that all students regardless of needs have a right to an education, and that parents must participate in any educational decision-making. Unlike the other social identities in this book, in the United States, parent advocacy is an expectation for students with special needs. While parents are likely aware that their country has laws to support children with needs, few are aware of the intricacies. Parents don't always understand how these laws pertain to their child or how the school determines exactly what their child's needs are and creates a plan to address this.

In Luelmo and Kasari (2021), the authors examined the effectiveness of a specific educational intervention designed for Latinx parents with children with needs. The intervention in this study had two goals. The first was to increase parent understanding of the special education system and the second was to increase parent advocacy. The authors discovered that when parents exited the program, they had a better understanding of the special education system; however, they did not gain the confidence to advocate for their student (Luelmo and Kasari, 2021). Knowledge alone is not enough.

Parents, of course, learn as they work with their child's school. But in addition to understanding their child's specific needs and their rights under the law, parents need to feel comfortable with and respected by school employees in order to effectively advocate for their child's needs. We will discuss the role of relationships in parent advocacy in the next section.

Sometimes parents are surprised by, or in denial of, their child's diagnosis. Other times, parents suspect something is going on for their child and are struggling toward a deeper understanding. When Cassie attended her son's Back-to-School Night, she viewed his work alongside that of his peers. She was struck by the difference and contacted the teacher the next day. Her son's teacher was resistant to her questions, seemingly acknowledging a problem while simultaneously refusing to address Cassie's questions.

Eve knew that Toby was different from his peers. Beginning in preschool, she suspected he might be on the autism spectrum. For Toby, everything came to a head in third grade, when his behavior began to stand out significantly and disrupt the classroom. Eve recognized her good fortune, noting that she did not need to educate her son's teachers about best practices for students with autism spectrum disorder or convince Ms Shah that Toby needed specialized intervention rather than discipline.

Eve's experience was markedly different from that of Cassie. Instead, the educators at Toby's school already had the knowledge and the resources to work with students on the spectrum. Toby's teacher immediately implemented processes to support Toby, even before his IEP was in place. Unlike Cassie, Eve was not alone in advocating for her child. Additionally, Emily and Lewis's experiences differ from that of Eve. Like Cassie, Emily brought questions to Lewis's teacher. However, in Lewis's case, the school did want to intervene with a plan, however, their plan focused on behavior and did not explore any other possible reasons for Lewis's struggles at school.

Deepen your practice

1. Compare Mrs Jordan and her response to that of Ms Shah. What similarities do you notice? Differences? How might each teacher's response impact a parent's understanding of their child's diagnosis?
2. List the actions Ms Shah took which created a positive outcome for Toby. Which of these actions do you think were most important, and why? What else could Ms Shah have done?

Advocacy and relationships

A special education diagnosis impacts the ways in which parents relate to others. As a metasynthesis of qualitative evidence noted (conducted by Samsell et al., 2022), parents of students with needs may experience emotional upheaval which spans anxiety, fear, and depression. Parents also report feelings of grief, guilt, and isolation from family and friends who cannot relate to their experiences. And while the study referenced above focused specifically on a diagnosis of autism spectrum disorder, this is true of other diagnoses as well. Two challenges in particular impact relationships with a family's community: (1) the stigma and judgment which frequently accompany parenting a child in special education; and (2) the work required to manage relationships with their child's school.

Stigma and judgment

Parents often report feeling judged and stigmatized by others, including their extended family, the community, and even their child's school. These feelings complicate the already complex world of special education (Samsell et al., 2022). Cassie's experience at Back-to-School Night is one example. The placement of Joseph's desk away from the other desks indicated stigma, not only to Cassie but to the other parents as well. Cassie proceeded to advocate for her son in an emotionally fraught setting.

Likewise, Eve observed that "in our culture, we do not discern between nurture and nature. We think parents are able to control everything." She shared the judgment she felt from her extended family. "My four-year-old was having meltdowns everywhere" and my sister-in-law would repeat "We've never seen a kid like this. I would never let my kid act like this!" Judgment from family, friends, the school, and the community is emotionally painful because they assume "it's all your fault." Looking back at that incident, Eve laughed and asked, "Do we ever have that much control over another human being?"

School relationships

Advocating for a child with needs is exhausting, but critically important. Maintaining positive relationships within a school is central to achieving the best education for a student because receiving appropriate interventions in K-12, and especially in K-6 education, can have an impact on a child's future. For example, Kat, a suburban parent in the northeast of the United States, knew from both talking with her friends in a Down syndrome community and from doing her own reading that many children with Down syndrome could successfully learn to read. She brought this idea to her daughter's school system and asked that they increase their efforts, in part because better reading skills would translate into greater independence for her daughter Elizabeth as an adult.

The special education staff shared their satisfaction with the current reading program. Kat had a choice: should she acquiesce to the school and risk Elizabeth not developing as high a reading level as needed? Or should she object and advocate for increased attention to reading which would potentially damage her primarily positive relationship with her daughter's team? In the end, Kat did neither. Instead, she created a group outside of school and hired a teacher. Thanks to Kat's family resources, Elizabeth's reading improved.

Families bring common priorities to their school relationship: "establish[ing] positive relationships, maintain[ing] positive relationships" and "avoid[ing] the damage of negative relationships on their child and on them" (Buren, Rios, and Burke, 2021, p. 16). Both Kat's and Cassie's stories demonstrate the intense emotional work parents put into managing relationships with schools. Since these relationships pivot on very serious subject matters, child well-being both in the present and for the future, they are naturally contentious at times. In fact, schools pay a steep price for ignoring family-school relationships. According to Muller et al. (2008), failure to attend to relationships with families in the special education process costs money. School districts across the United States were found to have spent a total of more than $146 million in conflict resolution (Mueller, 2008, p. 288).

Parents of children with special needs recognize that they must maintain a delicate balance in their relationships with school employees. They must advocate sufficiently to assure their child's needs are met, but not so forcefully, or so frequently, that staff see them as a problem. Once a parent oversteps, the relationship deteriorates and the parent's ability to effectively advocate for change diminishes. Cassie believed she overstepped the line by demanding an evaluation, thereby damaging her relationships with school staff. This bind leads parents to feel as though they are unable to advocate for their children without jeopardizing their relationships with school personnel (Buren, Rios, and Burke, 2021).

Eve believed that her positive relationships with her sons' teachers lightened the emotional burden of parenting two children with significant needs. She shared that her sons' teachers regularly told her that she was a good parent and acknowledged that her children were exhausting to parent. As she picked up her sons, they told her, "You are doing such a good job" and "I can't imagine how hard your weekends are." These comments validated Eve's experiences. She felt understood because the teachers were "some of the few people who really understand what is going on in our house—no one else gets how atypical it is, how hard it is." In turn, she regularly reciprocated appreciation for the teachers and school staff, for example, surprising them with goodie bags.

By contrast, Emily's relationship with school staff deteriorated completely. Trust was broken when, first, Lewis was labeled as "a troublemaker" and "stubborn and difficult," and second when these deficit views interfered with getting real help. Emily pulled Lewis out of school rather than allow him to be submitted to the unfair judgment of his teachers and special education liaisons.

Deepen your practice

- **"Give the kid a break, give the parent a break"**—Eve notes that the emotional impact of a special education diagnosis makes everything harder for parents and for the child. She cautions against assuming anything about the child or parent. You never know what a family is facing at home, and you never know how a child's path will unfurl in the future. Regarding her younger son, she states, "[He] has a pretty good chance of getting into serious trouble at some point and I'm right here—I'm doing my best." Give parents a chance to prove themselves.
- Over the next month, pay attention to the parents and children you see at work or in your regular life. Watch for parents struggling with their child.
    - First, note your immediate reaction. Do you think, "I would never let my child do that!" or "She's a terrible mother"?
    - Next, note the basic facts of the situation. What is the child doing? What is the parent doing?

- o Now, "give the parent a break." What else might be going on here? What other explanations exists for the behaviors you've witnessed?

- Look back at the vignettes. Which teacher actions built stronger school-family relationships? Which actions broke these relationships? Put yourself in the place of any teacher in this chapter. Write what you would do in the same way as that teacher and explain what you would do differently.

Impact of resources on parent advocacy

Families with children with special needs have different kinds and different amounts of resources. Resources can be defined as any attribute which provides a family with more educational options for their student; for example, Kat's ability to hire a reading teacher and create a group. In Eve's case, her part time job offered flexibility and time which she used to confer with teachers and manage Toby's education. Two types of resources impact parent advocacy in special education: family resources and school and district resources. Resources include everything from family income, to experience with advocacy in other areas, to the amount of free time parents have to devote to their child's needs. Each of these, among other resources, drive the amount of control a family has over a special needs child's education. Resources determine the extent to which parents are dependent on a school for support and whether the school is the sole or primary provider of educational interventions. Finances are a critical consideration because a special needs diagnosis can be very expensive. Students may need outside testing, tutors, in-home supports, advocates to support parent work with the school system, or specific medical treatment including medicines, therapies, or surgeries.

In the United States, there are few consistent, federal expectations around how states should support families. For example, rural districts tend to have fewer resources for children with needs than suburban and urban districts (Buren, Rios, and Burke, 2021). Massachusetts, in FY21, spent about 22 percent of total, direct, educational funds on special education (Massachusetts Department of Elementary and Secondary Education, 2022). Conversely, in 2004, Texas capped any district's special education population at 8.5 percent of the total student population. This reduced the amount of money the state spent on special education. Unfortunately, it also meant that some children did not receive appropriate education and, in particular, "students with mild impairments who couldn't get access to special education were much less likely to graduate from high school or go to college" (Hart, 2019). The *Houston Chronicle* exposed this practice in an investigative series in 2016 which brought an end to the 8.5 percent cap of special education students, but not before damaging the educational prospects of tens of thousands of students (*Houston Rosenthal*, 2016). Given such variation, a family's access to resources is central to **how** they advocate and **what** they advocate for (Buren, Rios, and Burke, 2021).

The intensity of parent advocacy sometimes reflects the resources available to the family both personally and through the school or community. For example, Emily, a single mom to three and also low-income, pulled her son from school when the school saw deliberate misbehavior while Emily saw ADHD. She quit her job and spent six months finding free community resources to get the diagnosis and support Lewis needed. Once she became aware that her son's school would be unwilling to treat her son's underlying condition, she acted.

The vignettes featured in this chapter stood out because two of the mothers were white, highly educated, and had significant family resources. Eve worked as a lawyer, although at less than half time. Her husband was a software engineer, and they had family resources including one full-time salary, a partial salary through Eve's work, a house they owned, education, and supportive family in the area. Moreover, given that Eve worked part-time, she was able to advocate for her children while also "working closely with the school and teachers." With a full-time job, she would not have been able to do so. Eve points out two resources, in particular, that have been central to her family's successful navigation of her son's neurodiversity: family resources and school resources. Even so, despite her greater familiarity with the law, Eve still found her special education journey bewildering and stressful at times. She says, "I'm overwhelmed and I'm a freakin' lawyer!"

Likewise, Cassie's family had financial resources, and her expertise was in writing and communication. Cassie was comfortable consulting with lawyers and penning a letter she drily described as "not friendly." Nonetheless, that advocacy disrupted her relationship with her son's elementary school. Lastly, Emily's case reveals the complex ways in which ability and race intersect. In Lewis's case, race and ability were interwoven when racial stereotypes around the behavior of Black boys took precedence over an actual diagnosis. Furthermore, Emily's position, as a single mother earning a low income, also influenced her relationship with her son's team. Moreover, "data on the income and education levels of parents were extracted where available, but the majority of studies did not provide this information" (Samsell et al., 2022, p. 95). Therefore, relationships with families in special education need to use diverse methods of engagement and maintain awareness of the complexity of family contexts. Schools can no longer use a one-size-fits-all approach. Instead, we must respect and acknowledge the diversity of our school populations and adapt our practices to the background of parents as well as to the breadth of diagnoses.

Samsell et al. (2022) also conclude that feeling empowered to advocate may also divide along racial and ethnic lines. However, they remark that there is not enough research into the impact of race and ethnicity on special education in general to draw conclusions. In Chapter 1, there are echoes of this in the advocacy experiences of Emily and Angela. Both Emily, a white mother advocating for her Black son, and Angela, a Latinx mother advocating for her teen son, find themselves in an environment which devalues their views.

Deepen your practice

- At your setting, ask if anyone has created a resource list for families coming to terms with their students' needs. Will the resources help them gain knowledge about their child's diagnosis? About their child's right by law? If yes—what's included and what's missing? If no, survey your colleagues and compile resources to meet this need.
- How might parent income and parent education influence a child's journey through special education? How might

parent experiences differ by income? By education level? By language? By race/ethnicity?

Chapter discussion questions

As teachers, we have the ability to reduce the emotional toll on parents with a child or children with needs. Review the list of possible actions:

- o   Making the process transparent
- o   Learning and implementing conflict resolution
- o   Opening lines of communication
- o   Expanding your knowledge of the special education system in your setting and create a guide for parents
- o   Asking families what they need.

Choose one of the actions listed above and describe how you might implement this in your classroom. Or take an existing classroom practice and extend it or deepen it. How might these changes support children and/or their parents?

Extension activities

- Interview a parent who has a child with needs. How do they feel about their school's special education process? Did they find it transparent and easy to understand? Have they advocated for their child? If so, how and for what?"
- What is the special education process like in your setting? What range of disabilities does your school serve? Look at the school and/or district's website. Is it easy to find information about special education? If you were a parent, could you find

the information you needed? Does the process seem clear and transparent? What do you think is missing?

3
Gender identity
"Will my child be OK in this school?"

Chapter learning objectives

Gain clarity about the lived experiences of students who are gender diverse and understand the significant and sometime dangerous challenges students and families face daily.

Introduction

In the past 20 years, awareness of LGBTQ+ issues has increased rapidly, and with this, public views of those in the LGBTQ+ community have also evolved rapidly. Two notable examples are the *Obergefell v. Hodges* 2015 Supreme Court decision granting the right of marriage to gay and lesbian couples and, in North Carolina, the passing (2016) and subsequent repeal (2017) of HB2 (The Bathroom Bill), which restricted use of public bathrooms to one's sex assigned at birth. Support for people who are gay and lesbian has increased and same sex marriage, at the time of writing, remains legal. The same support has not been true for those identifying as transgender and nonbinary, and schools have become a battleground for this issue with ongoing and rancorous discourse about what should be taught, who can use bathrooms, and how to serve transgender and nonbinary students best. This chapter focuses on parent advocacy in schools for children who identify as transgender or nonbinary.

K-12 schools increasingly face students whose gender expression does not match their sex assigned at birth. These students and their families face many challenges, including a lack of institutional readiness to support, pushback from families and community members who believe LGBTQ+ issues have no place in schools, and increasing incidents of violence and bullying. Gender diverse members of the LGBTQ+ community face significant risks at school.

In general, students who identify as LGBTQ+ have higher incidences of mental health issues (Seager Van Dyk et al., 2022).However, when you focus solely on youth who identify as transgender or nonbinary, these rates increase significantly, and finally, people who identify as nonbinary not only experience the highest rates of harm, but they also experience "more adverse health outcomes compared to their cisgender and binary transgender counterparts" (Bull et al., 2022, p. 127).

However, "being LGBTQ+ doesn't cause mental health problems and is not caused by mental health problems" (Garey, 2022b). Instead, clinical psychologist Emma Woodward notes that children who are gender diverse may "experience severe distress that they associate with the gender they were assigned at birth. They know something is not right, and it's felt this way for a long time" (Miller, 2022). Risk arises not from their gender identity but from "exposure to factors like rejection, bullying, discrimination, and violence" (Garey, 2022b). In fact, research indicates that the suicide rate plummets when transgender teens have access to gender-affirming health care.

Students who identify as LGBTQ+ report high levels of marginalization, including both physical threat and physical harm, and both in-person and online bullying. LGBTQ+ youth (ages 13–24) are four times more likely to attempt suicide than their peers, at a rate of one attempt every 45 seconds. Thus, school attention to the safety, well-being, and education of LGBTQ+ students should be of paramount importance because "the effects of a negative school environment are long-lasting and compounding," and students who are bullied at school are less likely to be successful across multiple measures (Orr and Baum,p. 11).

The topic of gender identity is contentious in the United States, so parent advocacy for their gender diverse children is equally controversial. As a framework for this chapter, I'd like to set forth a few basic understandings:

Gender continuum—Gender is not determined by one's biology. Instead, ideas about gender emerge from tacit societal agreements; for example, asserting that girls like pink or that boys like trucks. In actuality, gender can be seen as a continuum, with some folks comfortable with either the male or female sides. Others, however, find themselves somewhere in the middle, identifying as both male and female, or not on the continuum, identifying as neither male nor female. These people identify as nonbinary. People who are transgender find themselves placed on the wrong end of the continuum and work to become fully themselves by moving to the end which matches their true gender.

Sexuality, sex, and gender—Sexuality refers to attraction, while gender refers to "the interior experience of being a man, a woman, a nonbinary person, or otherwise" (The Trevor Project, 2022a). Sex, by contrast, is the "classification of a person as male, female, or intersex … typically based solely on one's genitals" (The Trevor Project, 2022a). For example, in the article *Parent advocacy for transgender and gender-expansive youth*, Stark (2022) notes that her child "Marie, describes her gender as who she is 'on the inside'" (p. 144). Marie was assigned to be male at birth, and "on the inside" is female. Likewise, Chaz Bono states "there's a gender in your brain and a gender in your body. For 99 percent of people, those things are in alignment. For transgender [and nonbinary] people, they're mismatched. That's all it is" (Orr and Baum, p. 8). In the cases of people who are nonbinary or transgender, "sex does not equal gender" (The Trevor Project, 2021).

A professional ethic of care—Teachers have a unique responsibility to their students. The Trevor Project (2022a) points out that "Every student has the right to learn in a safe and accepting school environment" (p. 3). The Human Rights Campaign notes that teachers have "professional ethic of care," which is a mandate to "ensure that every child feels safe and affirmed in their classroom." Educators routinely work with children and families from varied backgrounds, holding diverse beliefs and values. It is impossible to agree with every family's position. Therefore, "all adults must act as protective agents committed to the safety and well-being of the youth they serve" (p. 3).

Educators do not have to change their core beliefs to work with transgender and nonbinary students, but they may not impose their own values on a child or family because "it is irrelevant whether a person's objection to a student's identity or expression is based on sincerely held religious beliefs or the belief that the student lacks the capacity or ability to asset their gender identity or expression" (Orr and Baum, p. 3). What matters is the experience of the child in our classroom. We cannot run our classrooms as if certain students simply do not exist. Transgender and nonbinary students **do** exist, and they deserve equal footing in the classroom.

Language—Language preferred by the LGBTQ+ community changes over time as societal understandings change and deepen. At the writing of this book, I've chosen to use the terms gender identity, nonbinary, and transgender throughout this chapter, understanding that these terms will likely evolve over time and, at some point, may cease to be current or appropriate. Ultimately, as Stark indicates, "the language used to describe the LGBTQ+ community is ever evolving. In all instances, it is the members of the LGBTQ+ community who define what these terms mean to them" (Stark, 2022, p. 147).

Vocabulary

Cisgender—"people whose gender identity aligns with the sex they were assigned at birth" (The Trevor Project, 2022a).
Transgender—"people whose gender identity differs from the sex they were assigned at birth" (The Trevor Project, 2022a).
Nonbinary—"people who experience their gender identity and/or expression as outside of the male-female gender binary." Other terms include, but are not limited to "genderfluid, genderqueer, polygender, bigender, demigender, and agender" (The Trevor Project, 2022a).

Gender expression—"the way in which [people] present or express [their] gender, including physical appearance, clothing, hairstyles, and behavior" (The Trevor Project, 2022a).

Vignettes

Note: The following stories are not real. In this chapter, the vignettes are composite examples rather than anonymized stories of real people. Parents with transgender and nonbinary children were not comfortable having their stories published, even after anonymization, because of the risks associated with discovery.

Kit, Geoff, and Leah's story

Kit's parents, Geoff and Leah, knew from the time Kit was in preschool that they were not like their peers. Assigned female at birth, Kit clearly had different ideas about how they should present in public. Dressing for school was always a struggle. Kit routinely rejected any and all "girl" clothing (pink, purple, ruffled, skirted…). Picture days in elementary school were particularly fraught. Geoff and Leah requested Kit wear a fancy dress and ribbons in their hair. Kit refused. Additionally, Kit constantly lobbied for a short haircut. Leah encouraged Kit to keep their hair long because her own parents never allowed her to have long hair. Exhausted by these battles, Kit's parents sought help. They spoke with doctors, educators, religious leaders, fellow parents, and family members. However, they discovered that, while other parents had similar battles, Kit's intensity was greater. Moreover, Geoff and Leah's boundaries regarding Kit's appearance seemed to make things worse rather than better.

By fourth grade, Kit was adamant that they weren't a girl or a boy. Leah began to concede and told Kit that they "could be themselves in a way that was quiet and less obvious." She encouraged Kit to choose clothing that met this goal, suggesting, for example, a black shirt with a scoop neck, and a salmon shirt from the boy's department. She automatically vetoed rainbow clothing saying, "that's not who we are." Leah came to regret this approach stating, "I wish I could go back to grade 4 and do things differently."

In fifth grade, Kit's anxiety about school and their appearance became pronounced. They developed a distinct eye tic, reoccurring nightmares, and terrible stomachaches. By October, Kit was lethargic, morose, and sporadically refused to go to school. Clearly something was very, very wrong. Geoff and Leah were split. Leah wanted to allow Kit to cut their hair, to dress as they pleased, and to explore what lay beneath these behaviors. Geoff did not. He believed they should "hold firm" because, as he frequently said, "your gender is what's in your pants."

Leah was racked by guilt, worry, and indecision. While Geoff felt Kit was "only ten and would change their mind," Leah was less sure. On her own, she found The Trevor Project and connected with people in the local LGBTQ+ community. With their support, she was better able to support Kit. In turn, Kit turned toward Leah and started avoiding Geoff.

However, one day, Geoff discovered that Leah had been taking Kit to a local group for LGBTQ+ youth and insisted she stop. A terrible argument followed. The next day at school, Kit moved forward on their own. At recess, they stood at the top of the play structure at recess and told their classmates to call them Kit and use they/them pronouns. Later that day, they snuck into the school bathroom and cut their hair short. Kit's teacher called the family and set up a meeting.

Looking back, Leah saw this as a pivot point. That afternoon, Leah and Geoff met with the school and were offered a transition plan for Kit. Leah agreed. Geoff became livid and accused the school, and Leah, of indoctrinating Kit and ruining their life. He stormed away in the middle of the meeting. When he returned that evening, he had bags full of feminine clothing in Kit's size. He ordered Kit to change immediately saying, "You just have to get used to being a girl. Your mother has let you get away with this ridiculousness. People are girls or boys—there's nothing else. Change now."

Kit refused and burst into tears. Leah had an epiphany. She realized that being neither a girl nor a boy was somehow integral to Kit's well-being. She said, "I realized this was not about me or my beliefs—this was actually about Kit and right now Kit needed their mom to fully and completely support them. Geoff's position was so rigid and unkind, he was going to break my child. He was going to break my baby. I decided right then that I wasn't going to lose Kit. No matter how uncomfortable I was, I had to put Kit's needs first."

That night, Geoff and Leah separated, and Geoff moved out. Leah and Kit worked with the school on a transition plan which went smoothly until the other parents heard. Leah notes, "The minute we announced Kit's transition plan to the other families, I lost all my friends. They deserted us. We had no one."

Alex, Rich, and Willa's story

Alex and parents Rich and Willa's journey began when Alex was in eighth grade. From Willa and Rich's perspective, Alex never seemed to fit in. He had a small group of friends, but he and his friends were regularly called names, harassed in the hallways, and bullied on social media. Alex, designated female at birth, became highly anxious and began cutting. He spent six weeks in an inpatient psychiatric unit and began to work with a therapist. In April, Alex sent Willa and Rich an email explaining that he was male, not female and that he hoped his parents would still love him.

Willa had friends whose children had transitioned and always felt comfortable with the idea. But Alex's email stunned her. "I was having trouble understanding what I was reading. I was so overwhelmed I just burst into tears of worry, stress and sadness." However, she knew Alex needed support immediately. "I knew instinctively that his worries about coming out to us were more important than my mini breakdown. I wiped my tears and went directly to his room to hug him."

Rich, Willa, and Alex agreed that Alex would start high school as himself—presenting as male. In preparation, they sought the help of friends, met with Alex's pediatrician, and had a series of meetings with the high school administration. The family headed into August feeling optimistic. Alex felt ready. He knew he'd be in classes with friends from elementary and middle school and the school seemed aware of the problems Alex might face.

Despite this, ninth grade was rocky. His former friends passed him in the hall and averted their eyes, pretending not to see him. When he sat next to them at lunch, they got up and moved. In class, they interacted with him as little as possible. Alex felt simultaneously invisible and contagious. Moreover, some students publicly shamed him. One senior boy bellowed a homophobic slur to him every single day on the way to the cafeteria and everyone else laughed. Alex solved this problem by taking the long way and avoiding him. In another painful incident, a longtime family friend (buddies since age three) stopped him in the hall and called him by his birth name. She raised her voice and asked, "Why do you dress that way? Why can't you be normal?" With that, she turned and walked away, leaving a circle of students frozen and staring at Alex.

Moreover, this large, suburban high school employed no visibly nonbinary or transgender adults. The curriculum only mentioned these identities in health class. Even then, they were only defined and never discussed. His teachers never even hinted that gender diverse students attended this school. The single "all gender" bathroom was located in the basement and was quite a walk from the main portions of the building. It was also located next to the girl's locker room. He frequently found members of PE classes and, after school, the Varsity Cheer Team using the bathroom to change. Once, Alex asked them to use the locker room instead, explaining, "Hey, this is the only bathroom in the school that I can use and I'm going to be late to my next class." The student replied, "I can use this bathroom. I'm female and that's a gender." After accumulating a series of tardies caused by trips to the bathroom, Alex simply reduced the amount he drank during the day and waited until he got home to use the bathroom.

Rich and Willa approached the high school about the negative school climate and outlined the impact it was having on their son. They were concerned for his safety, his physical and mental health, and his academic progress. Through a series of meetings, Rich and Willa learned that the school was aware and supportive, in theory. Teachers were supposed to use a child's preferred pronouns, the administration was expanding the curriculum to be more inclusive, the school had an active GSA with a supportive and well-loved adviser, and overall, the educators believed they were adequately meeting the needs of transgender and nonbinary students.

However, when asked about increasing the number of "all gender" bathrooms and addressing the ongoing bullying, the principal responded that bathrooms were part of the district's seven-year plan and would be completed in year five, which of course, would be the year **after** Alex's graduation. Bullying, they noted, was an ongoing problem for many students, but they had planned professional development at the end of the year to specifically explore bullying of LGBTQ+ students. In other words, the school had no plans to take immediate action in support of Alex.

That night, Rich and Willa discussed the disconnect between the school's understanding of their son's experiences and Alex's everyday, on the ground life at school. If Alex stayed at the school, he would have limited access to the bathroom and would continue to handle bullying on his own. Furthermore, anti-transgender protests were popping up locally. These protests featured statements such as "children are never born in the wrong body." These ideas stood in stark contrast to Alex's experiences and were in complete opposition to their own values. With anti-transgender sentiment on the rise in their community and with the school's lack of urgency, they began to fear that Alex's school could not actually keep him safe.

Reflection

- What impact do you think Geoff's and Leah's different views have on Kit? On the school?
- What would you do if you were in Willa and Rich's situation?
- If Alex were in your class and you observed the treatment described above, what would you do?

Research is clear that parental support of transgender and nonbinary students is critical to both student well-being and student success. Parental acceptance and support results in fewer mental health and related issues for students and leads to better school success (Abreu et al., 2019; Bull et al., 2022; Seager Van Dyk et al., 2022). When schools and parents work together, children fare even better. Therefore, parent advocacy in schools has become critical to the success and safety of their students. Schools need to know how to support not only the students but also the parents.

Parent advocacy for child transgender and nonbinary gender identities is marked by a few important characteristics. For the purpose of this chapter, we'll look at three parent responses to a child coming out as nonbinary or transgender. First, parents must come to terms with the idea that their child's gender identity does not match their sex assigned at birth. Next, parents adapt. During this stage, parents begin to gather information and connect with others on the same path. In many cases, they begin to change their beliefs. Finally, this journey ends in advocacy for their (and other) gender diverse children.

Coming out and coming to terms

"It's kind of impossible for a child to be private about their gender. For one thing, they can't just pick up and move to a different state and start a new life… ." In their hometown, "invariably, if it's not obvious, kids will bluntly ask, 'are you a boy or a girl?'" (Sirois, 2020). This comment from Martie Sirois, parent to a transgender child, encapsulates the difficulty parents face in coming to terms with their child's gender identity in their own communities. Not only is a child's transition publicly visible, but schools also use gender frequently as a way to sort and organize children. Teachers ask students to line up boy/girl and hand out bathroom passes to the boys' or girls' restrooms. Sirois notes that these experiences are "brutal reminders that [a student's] gender identity doesn't matter—or worse—doesn't exist."

Gender identity is a contentious topic in the United States. Given that coming out as nonbinary or transgender frequently involves a noticeable change, the process is marked by deep, and often public, scrutiny. Moreover, transgender and nonbinary children are not necessarily seen as children. Instead, their lives become proxy for "a political or social issue" (Stark, 2022, p. 149) and the children themselves are obscured. Unsurprisingly, parents of transgender and nonbinary children face similar obstacles as they navigate their child's identity, and these obstacles influence how parents advocate and how they develop a family-school relationship (Sirois, 2020).

Adjusting and adapting

Parents frequently describe this as a "dynamic 'journey'" (Gray et al., 2015, p. 129). However, since parents are informed by their own "familial and cultural" context (p. 125), they approach their child's gender identity in distinct ways. No two journeys are the same. Like Geoff and Leah, often parents first notice behavior from their child which challenges gender norms. While some of these behaviors are age-appropriate, students like Kit may show persistence and intensity over time, which distinguishes them from their peers.

Abreu et al.'s (2019) literature review, regarding parental reactions to children who are transgender or nonbinary, asserts that as parents come to terms with the idea that their child does not embrace the sex assigned at birth, they experience a combination of deep and powerful emotions ranging from "grief and loss" for the future they imagined, to "strong, positive, loving reactions," and even, "traumatic shock" (p. 476). At the same time, many parents also confront and struggle with their deeply held beliefs and values by coming face to face with their own prejudices (Abreu et al., 2019; Bull et al., 2022).

Neither Geoff nor Leah was comfortable with the idea of transgender and nonbinary people. When Kit declared themself, both parents faced a clash between their values and their love for their child. Leah adapted, while Geoff remained steadfast in his belief that "gender is what's in your pants." Moreover, their turmoil was heightened because they no longer fitted neatly into their extended family and community. Families who are predominantly accepting also grieve (Abreu et al., 2019).

Acceptance of youth who identify as transgender or nonbinary varies from outright rejection to enthusiastic acceptance. For many children, rejection results in homelessness. According to The Trevor Project (2022b), "homelessness and housing instability were reported at higher rates among transgender and nonbinary youth, including 38% of transgender girls/women, 39% of transgender boys/men, and 35% of nonbinary youth." Among the remaining children, Gray et al. (2015) found that parents initially either accepted or rescued their child. Acceptance of a child was marked by a shift toward understanding and accommodating a child's needs, while rescuing parents tried to change their child. Parent responses, in part, were determined by how parents viewed gender. If parents believed that gender is binary and a choice, they were more likely to rescue their child. One parent in Gray et al.'s (2015) study described this dynamic as "editing." She stated, "he's so good at editing himself now… I think [editing] is just a reality" (p. 130). Essentially, rescuing requires a child to suppress or edit out the parts of themselves which do not align to societal expectations. Predictably, rescuing frequently results in power struggles and conflict between parent and child.

Leah and Geoff both tried to rescue Kit. For example, Leah negotiated with Kit around clothing, telling Kit that they "could be themselves in a way that was quiet and less obvious." She shopped with Kit for clothing that met this goal, a black shirt with a scoop neck, a salmon shirt from the boys department. Leah came to regret this approach stating, "I wish I could go back to grade 4 and do things differently." Geoff attempted to rescue Kit by forcing them to present as female in the belief that Kit would eventually adjust to a female presentation. Both Leah and Geoff were asking Kit to edit themself.

In comparison, Willa and Rich accepted Alex immediately. They knew transgender and nonbinary people and sought support from others who had been on this journey. Once they understood the root of Alex's depression, they worked to meet his needs. Even so, Willa's responses were emotionally intense and variable. "I was having trouble understanding what I was reading. I was so overwhelmed I just burst into tears of worry, stress, and sadness."

Overall, acceptance of a nonbinary or transgender child depends on learning and parent connection with LGBTQ+ communities. When parents connect with LGBTQ+ communities, acceptance of their child may increase (Abreu et al., 2019). For example, the more Leah learned, the more open she became to Kit's expressed gender. Therefore, acceptance and rescue exist on a continuum, with many parents moving from a rescue approach to one of acceptance.

Lastly, this part of the parent journey does not touch only parent and child. The whole family must adapt, and inevitably, this process changes family relationships. One key point of conflict is the parents. While Willa and Rich were aligned regarding Alex's transition, Leah and Geoff were not. Their disagreement about how best to support Kit layered another significant stressor on an already challenging family situation. The impact of Leah and Geoff's split was far-reaching. Kit grew closer to their mother and distant from their father. and this tension ended in separation.

Likewise, siblings and extended family members react to a child's identity. These reactions also ripple through the entire family. Older children may accept or rescue their sibling. Finally, the extended family, including grandparents, aunts, uncles, cousins, and more, also frequently struggle to accept a child's gender. (Gray et al., 2015), Leah and Kit lost not only Geoff's support, but also the support of, and connection to, Geoff's side of the family.

Deepen your practice

1. Take the parent's perspective. What might a rescuing parent want from a teacher or school? What might an accepting parent request?
2. What did your family of origin believe about gender? Are your adult beliefs in line with or different from those of your family? Spend five minutes outlining your current view of gender and how it is similar to and/or different from that of your family. How might these similarities and/or differences affect your work with transgender and nonbinary children? List five possible ways.
3. How can you manage a family-school relationship when parents disagree in the way Leah and Geoff do? In a group, discuss the ways in which you can center a child's needs without politicization. How can you center Kit's needs in the school regardless of adult emotions on this topic?

Parental transformation

Gathering information

As parents adjust to the idea that their child's gender identity may not match their sex at birth, many feel "overwhelmed by a lack of knowledge" (Abreu et al., 2019, p. 477). Information leads parents to a deeper understanding of the challenges gender diverse people face in the United States. Lastly, in some families, this awareness builds compassion. This transformation from adjusting to awareness to compassion is critical because parent support is a central mitigating factor in good mental health and each step of the process allows parents to better support their child (Seager Van Dyk et al., 2022). However, gathering information can be hard. Not all areas of the United States accept transgender and nonbinary individuals. Some have legislated against providing children with gender-affirming care, labeling such as child abuse. Other places have forbidden discussion of children who are transgender or nonbinary in the classroom. Online communities support both parents and children although, as a parent in Bull et al.'s (2022) study notes, "there were lots of books and stories online of how to help your kid transition from boy to girl, but what about when your kid is not a boy or a girl, or is a girl and a boy? It took a long time to find help with that" (p. 125).

Parents typically begin their search for information in the form of books, websites, and connections with local members of the LGBTQ+ community. This is true regardless of a parent's initial reaction to their child's gender identity. Seager Van Dyk et al. (2022) note that parental reactions to their child coming out as transgender or nonbinary fell into three categories: positive, mixed, or negative. Regardless of the initial response, all parents wanted support and information, but couldn't always find it and finally, the authors found that parents with negative reactions were the most likely to seek more information.

Access to information is critical to supporting students because, as parents find more information and support, they begin to "develop cognitive flexibility" (Abreu et al., 2019, p. 477). Three of the four parents in our vignettes fit this description. Leah, Willa, and Rich asked friends, family members, and medical professionals for advice when their child began to show signs of being gender diverse. Information was particularly important to Leah's transformation. In Leah's case, information changed her parenting by shifting her view of Alex's gender identity from a phase to acceptance of nonbinary people.

Facing stigma

Parental transformation is also challenging because it brings parents face to face with discrimination and judgment against gender diverse people. Social intolerance of nonbinary and transgender children exists in every part of life. In Bull et al.'s (2022) study, one mother described her search for information and support this way, "well first I did a bunch of stuff that didn't help [laughing] before I found anything that did. I contacted probably a dozen therapists and counselors… Some of the responses I got were just, you know, dismissive as in 'your child is too young, you are getting ahead of yourself'. And one professional said, 'how did you do this to your child'!" (p. 133).

Discrimination also upends previously solid relationships with extended family and friends and their community, and institutional relationships with teachers, medical personnel, religious leaders, and elected leaders. Not only do these relationships change but parents are also subjected to severe judgments about their child and about their parenting. Unfortunately, sometimes relationships break beyond repair, leaving parents with minimal support. For example, at that pivotal moment in the fall of Kit's fifth grade year, Leah lost all support, friends, family members, and even her husband.

The level of social intolerance that parents and children experience is high and challenging to navigate. Intolerance impedes the process of transformation and amplifies the already existing stressors in a family. Leah and Geoff's marriage buckled under the strain of their disagreement. Alex's return to high school was stressful in its own right. The discrimination Alex experienced only added to his, and his family's, stress. In addition to adjusting to high school level classes and finding his way around a large building, Alex had to navigate a lack of bathrooms, threats to his safety, loneliness, and bullying from both strangers and childhood friends.

Compassion

The process of "developing awareness of discrimination" is a key part of parental transformation (Abreu et al., 2019, p. 478) and leads to deeper compassion for one's child. Hearing a child's stories of exclusion and discrimination inspires a parent to action and to deeper and more critical evaluation of both their child's experience in the schools and of their own parenting missteps. Stark (2022), in her autoethnography, observes, "Looking back, I now see how my behavior communicated rejection; Marie knew herself then, and my attempt to protect her from others' bigotry only invalidated her and made it impossible for her to present as her authentic self" (p. 146). Likewise, Leah looks back on her responses to Kit's request to cut their hair with remorse saying, "I loved Kit's long and thick brown hair. It was down to their waist and gorgeous. But I should have let them cut it. It's their hair—and my rules made things much, much worse for them."

Supporting parent transformation supports children. Abreu et al. (2019) find that the parent-child relationship improves as parents created "new personal narratives" to explain their child's, and their own, journeys (p. 463). This affirmation of their child's self has two outcomes: parental advocacy in schools and parental questioning of how best to keep their child safe.

Deepen your practice

1. Make or improve upon a list of resources for families with gender diverse children. What resources might parents need?
2. How does your school setting handle students who are exploring, transitioning, or identifying as transgender or nonbinary? Look at the district website and find the pertinent policies. Is it easy to find information? Is the school's policy clear?
3. What do the following two quotes suggest about how schools should interact with gender diverse students and their parents? What do they suggest about how schools should approach this topic?
   (a) Michael Enenbach, MD: "It's really vital to have the support of the parents even if parents don't agree with [what] the child is saying or doing. That means explicitly letting your child know that you love them, accept them, and stand by them—even if you are confused or upset by the thoughts and feelings they're having" (Garey, 2022a).
   (b) "It's not the kid's responsibility to manage their parents' emotional responses" (Garey, 2022a).

Will my child be OK?

Gray et al. (2015) note that the acceptance of a child's gender identity "leads to [both] relief and connection but also stress" because parents perceive the danger and intolerance of the path ahead (p. 130). This realization results in parent agency and advocacy (Bull et al., 2022). In order to keep their children safe in a world filled with hatred for who their child is, parents understand that acceptance at home is not enough. However, given the fraught political nature of this subject, how and when to advocate is rarely clear. There is no guidebook which covers the variation in social acceptance and legal rulings from school to school, community to community, and state to state. And so, parents are constantly in a state of doubt, asking themselves, "Am I doing the right thing?" (Gray et al., 2015, p. 131).

Leah's advocacy for Kit is an example. She put aside her own upbringing once she realized that Kit's inability to express their gender identity was the cause of their depression. Once she understood that the full expression of Kit's gender was the solution and not the problem, she began to advocate for Kit—with Geoff and with the school. As one mother in Bull et al.'s (2022) study described, Leah "figured out how to get [her] head in the game in order to support [Kit] properly" (p. 137). It is a parent's job to help. Stark (2022) notes that "I came to understand that being an affirming parent requires some level of advocacy on behalf of your child, as it is not enough to provide safety and recognition at home" (p. 154). The risks at school are significant and if parents don't advocate for their student, no one else will.

Given current controversy around the acceptance of gender diverse students in school, parental advocacy is often spurred by a fundamental question: "Will [my] child be OK in this school setting?" (Bull et al., 2022, p. 136). Parent advocacy focuses on many areas including "educating teachers and school administrators about [gender diversity], modeling acceptance of the child in public, empowering the child to self-advocate, and creating a safe space in the home for… expression" (Gray et al., 2015, p. 132).

As seen in our vignettes, often parent advocacy occurs in direct response to events which are physically or psychologically harmful for their child. For example, Bull et al. (2022) describe an elementary class in which students repeatedly asked 11-year-old Wren "what are you really?" (p. 136) and Wren's teacher asks students to line up in a boy-girl pattern to see where Wren would go. While this teacher was superficially accepting of Wren, her classroom practices and her lack of understanding of the emotional toll they have on gender diverse kids causes parents to worry about the physical and emotional well-being of their children. Like Leah, Willa, and Rich, this parent advocated to protect their child from the constant barrage of everyday situations wearing her child down.

Leah's advocacy of Kit is aligned with the research. She initially resisted Kit's transition to nonbinary until she saw the immense negative impact on her child, at which point she put aside her own misgivings and "got her head in the game." With resistance coming from her own husband and from the parents of Kit's classmates, Leah recognized that simply telling Kit that they were wrong and forcing them to comply would only make things worse, not better.

Willa and Rich thought they had their head in the game. They met with high school administrators prior to Alex's ninth grade year and shared Alex's needs and their parental concerns. They asked hard questions and tried to anticipate and address potential problems. This preparation was not enough. Willa and Rich discovered that while the school stated a willingness to create an inclusive and welcoming space for gender diverse students, their actions did not match. The school's awareness of their gender diverse youth did not include the struggles students like Alex faced daily.

Like Leah, they are not sure Alex will be OK in his school—and now they must make decisions to best support and protect him. And thus, they have no choice but to advocate—their child's well-being is central to this. Without advocacy, harm is likely. However, this advocacy is exhausting. "Advocating with and on behalf of Marie at the school and district level was exhausting and overwhelming for me." (Stark, 2022, p. 155).

Deepen your practice

- Gender stereotypes exist in many forms in schools. For example, many teachers still line children up in boy/girl order. List at least five binary gender practices at school and, for each, rework it to be gender neutral.
- You are the parent of a nonbinary student in grade 8. Your child uses the restroom in the nurse's office as the result of a district-wide policy on trans and nonbinary children. However, your child's English teacher has hall passes only for "boys" and "girls." Every time your child needs to use the bathroom during English—they must choose a gender. You requested that the teacher create a third pass for nonbinary and trans students, but he shares that school policy states that only two students can be in the restrooms from one class at any time—one girl and one boy. This policy was put in place to manage mischief in the restrooms (water fights, throwing wet paper towels, etc.). His hands, he says, are tied.

What do you think is going on here? What would you do as a teacher? What do you think a parent would do?

Chapter discussion questions

- What are your experiences of gender? Think back to your childhood. Were there times you were very comfortable with your gender and with the expectations of your gender? Were there times you were not comfortable? Spend five minutes jotting down your memories and how they made you feel.
- The topic of gender identity in schools is contentious. In small groups, describe how you would handle the following situation: You are a third-grade teacher and in your classroom is a child who identifies as nonbinary. You have been weaving LGBTQ+ stories and historical and current day figures into your curriculum as part of your socioemotional curriculum. Your goal, and that of the school more broadly, is to integrate any and all transgender and nonbinary students seamlessly into classroom life. However, another parent approached you to complain about the "indoctrination" of her child.

    o How will you approach this situation? How might you include school and district leadership in this discussion?

Extension activity

Research policies regarding transgender and nonbinary students at your school setting. Start with the website. Is the information easy to find and easy to understand? Reflect on your observations.

   o If your school has a stated policy, reflect on the extent to which they follow it.

- o Do the policies support truly transgender and nonbinary children? Do students have experiences like those of Kit and Alex?
- o What would you add to create a safer, more welcoming, and more inclusive school?
- o List five actions you can take in your classroom to assure a safe and inclusive environment for transgender and nonbinary children.

4
High socioeconomic status

"C is for Community College."

Chapter learning objectives

Gain awareness of the ways in which families with high socioeconomic status advocate for their child's education and develop understanding of the ways this advocacy may reflect their specific social identity and may have negative, unintended consequences.

Introduction

In the preceding chapters, we have explored how parents with social identities stemming from their marginalization advocate for their children. In this chapter, by contrast, we focus on parents with a social identity stemming from high socioeconomic status. This status conveys privileges "including jobs, wages, education, housing, food services, medicine, and cultural definitions" (Senosy and Diangelo, 2017, p. 222). Families with a social identity of high socioeconomic status tend to share many characteristics. In addition to abundant resources, many, though not all, families with this identity are white. Systemic racism in the United States has provided white families with systematic and ongoing advantages. In *The Hidden Cost of Being African American*, Shapiro (2004) maps the impact the family wealth for white families, accrued over decades and centuries, provides each new generation with "head start assets" which provide for the creation of future wealth through high-quality higher education and down payments for home purchasing (p. 64). While this chapter focuses primarily on family resources, it is impossible to fully separate socioeconomic status from race.

The vignettes below offer insight into how parents with some of these characteristics may use their resources to advocate for their children's education. Each vignette focuses on the idea (shared by the parents and the schools their children attend) that mathematics is a key pathway to adult success, and each hint at the potential for unintentional negative consequences from this advocacy. This idea is common overall in the United States and especially pronounced in affluent communities. Math is a current flashpoint for parent anxiety over their children's education. In the United States, parents see headlines like "Why Do Americans Stink at Math?" (Green, 2014). Moreover, these messages are omnipresent. Parents from communities with median incomes see these ideas in the news. They are targeted by marketing for academic support and college admissions counseling, and they hear these ideas on the playground from other parents. Naturally, these ideas create anxiety that **all** children are failing.

The irony is that in public schools in higher income communities, student performance in mathematics is at the top both nationally and internationally and so these headlines don't necessarily apply. David Berliner sums up this dynamic succinctly in a Washington Post opinion piece with Valerie Strauss (2017). Citing international, national, and college admissions tests, he states that "as income increases per family from our poorest families (under the 25th percentile in wealth), to working class (26th to 50th percentile in family wealth), to middle class (51st to 75th percentile in family wealth), to wealthy (the highest quartile in family wealth), mean scores go up quite substantially." Nevertheless, parents with resources often focus their attention on their children's academic success in mathematics through advocacy—which occurs in two forms. First, they use family resources to supplement schooling and second, they work to influence the school to meet the specific needs of their child.

Unsurprisingly, a social identity marked by high socioeconomic status influences the family-school relationship in a number of ways (Cheadle and Amato, 2011; Dumais, Kessinger, and Ghosh, 2012; Hill and Taylor, 2004; Lareau and Shumar, 1996; Robinson and Harris, 2014). For example, in Chapter 1, we learned that teachers may have unconscious biases against Black and Hispanic children. A similar but reverse effect is present when schools interact with families with a background of high income. Research demonstrates that educators perceive parents and students from privileged backgrounds (who are often, but not always, white) more favorably than those from less privileged backgrounds (Dumais, Kessinger, and Ghosh, 2012). There are a few possible reasons that families with a high socioeconomic status have advantages over others. Families with resources share certain characteristics beyond financial advantages, including (but not limited to) increased opportunities to communicate with school employees due to high levels of job flexibility, higher education levels creating ease and confidence when conversing with authorities, and a deeper understanding of how the educational system works and how to use the system to advocate for their child (Horvat et al., 2003; Lareau and Shumar, 1996). Each of these advantages offers families the opportunity to use advocate for the needs of their own child.

Vignettes

Ben's story

It was a rainy summer day at an elementary engineering camp in an affluent suburb of a large northeastern city. Elementary engineering focuses on hands-on problem-solving of complex tasks, with a focus on iteration, learning from failures, and the engineering design process. Seven-year-old Ben and his teacher were building a construction paper tower, trying to build as high as possible using nothing but masking tape. The other nine campers were focused, building, and chatting. Soon, talk turned to after-school math programs, specifically Kumon and Russian Math. These programs are two of many tuition-based after-school math programs which promise parents acceleration in mathematics and therefore a better chance of success in life. Their approaches are typically traditional. Ben began to interview his camp mates: "Do you do Russian Math or Kumon?" he asked. To his shock, only one other student did any math program. Ben spluttered, indignant and confused, "But, but! You have to do extra math! If you don't do math you won't get into a good college and if you don't get into a good college, you won't have a good life!" This idea, perhaps adopted from Ben's family, had become a mantra, organizing a distasteful activity into a meaningful future. His discomfort with the idea that some children did not do extra math classes underscored his winner-takes-all rationale. His statement seemed emblematic of this community's intense focus on learning and, at $2,000 per school year for one hour a week, his parents could afford this extra instruction (Lee, 2020, p. 37).

Beth, Rose, and Shawn's story

Beth was a bouncy 12-year-old with long, straight, dark brown hair, pale skin, and freckles. Her parents, Rose and Shawn, both with MBAs, worked long hours in financial services and, by outward appearances, were very successful. They drove a Lexus and Mercedes, took vacations to Turks and Caicos, and hired a sitter to shepherd their two children to a variety of after-school and summer programming.

At her Girls in Engineering camp, Beth demonstrated a talent for problem-solving; for example, she took electronics parts and rigged up a fan run by a small solar panel. She also worked well with others, exhibiting a quiet leadership. Beth didn't "run the show," but when she spoke, everyone listened. However, every day at lunch, Beth left the group. She grabbed her lunch, chose a table away from her campmates, and opened a workbook. One day, her teacher, who the kids called Ms B, asked why she ate alone. Beth's face fell. "I have to finish three pages of math each day or I'm not allowed to attend my sleepaway camp — it's my favorite place and all my friends are going."

Ms B asked to see what kind of math she was working on, and Beth showed her a page of adding fractions. Flipping through, Ms B could see that the entire book was practice in arithmetic, rather than developing and using mathematical concepts. "Is it fun? Do you like math?" she asked Beth. "No—I know it's important for my future. I love science and I know have to do math but I kinda hate it. And I'm bad at it. But if I don't do this, I can't go to camp, *and* I won't be able to get a good job."(vignette adapted from Lee, 2020).

Shane, Ginny, and Patrick's story

On a warm, sunny day in a southern Californian private elementary school, Elsie, a first-grade teacher, was preparing for the first day of school. Families had been invited to stop by for an informal introduction and a chance to see their new classroom. Shane appeared in the doorway with his parents: Ginny, a stay-at-home parent, and Patrick, a lawyer. Shane, who was new to the school, entered slowly and looked around. By contrast, his parents barreled past him, their arms full of workbooks. As Shane wandered around his new classroom, Ginny plunked her stack of books on the table where the teacher was sitting. "Hi," she said. "We're here to let you know that Shane is gifted in math. All through kindergarten he did his math workbooks and now is able to do third grade math. He can multiply and do long division." Elsie picked up the top workbook and flipped through. Each page was painstakingly completed in handwriting which scrawled across the page. She thanked the parents and said she looked forward to working with Shane.

Three months later, Elsie had assessed and worked with all 24 students. Shane was an unusual case. Given an equation, he could solve it using paper and pencil through common formulas. However, as soon as he was asked to demonstrate or describe precisely what these formulas meant, he froze. Before long, any conceptual mathematics activity, for example, using manipulatives to show how many the 1 in 18 represented (correct answer—a group of 10), had Shane lying on the carpet in a ball complaining of a stomachache.

Ginny and Patrick attended numerous meetings and flatly rejected Elsie's position that Shane needed to build up his underlying conceptual understanding of the formulas he used. Instead, they held a series of private meetings for parents from all first-grade classes. Later that fall, a group of parents led by Ginny approached Elsie after school, and forcefully advocated for more traditional mathematics instruction. They listed their demands, listed the perceived deficits in Elsie's (and the other) classrooms, and set an ultimatum: Teach "better" or we'll get you fired. Elsie involved the school administration and as promised, they shared their complaints, accused Elsie of incompetence, and tried to get her fired. However, the school administration sided with Elsie. Ginny and Patrick immediately pulled Shane from the school.

Ryan's story

Ryan is father to two elementary-aged children and lives in the suburb of a mid-Atlantic city. Their community has a renowned public school system which routinely ranks in the top ten of their state. Real estate is pricey with the median house selling at nearly two million dollars. Many families purchased homes in this town simply to have access to the school system. Ryan and his wife have PhDs. His is in a STEM field and, when it comes to math instruction, he is comfortable supplementing the school's curriculum. Ryan also notes that parents in his community "tell a story that they want their kids to acquire a love of [math] and achieve their potential" because they worry that "the school is not pushing them in the sense that they want [their kids] to achieve academically." Parents "feel very strongly about it." When asked whether these students did, in fact, develop a love of math, he answered, "No—the parents are like, we don't care, we're going to do it."

Vocabulary

Privilege—"The rights, advantages, and protections enjoyed by some at the expense of and beyond the rights, advantages, and protections available to others" (Senosy and Diangelo, 2017, p. 81).

Class—"The system of relative social rank as measured in terms of income, wealth, status, and/or power" (Senosy and Diangelo, 2017, p. 160). Concepts of class are social constructs.

Classism—"The systematic oppression of poor and working people by those who control resources (including jobs, wages, education, housing, food services, medicine, and cultural definitions). There are economic, political, and cultural dimensions to class" (Senosy and Diangelo, 2017, p. 222).

Socioeconomic status—"The position of an individual or group on the socioeconomic scale, which is determined by a combination of social and economic factors such as income, amount and kind of education, type and prestige of occupation, place of residence, and—in some societies or parts of society—ethnic origin or religious background" (APA Dictionary).

Reflection

Before we take a deeper look at these vignettes, consider the following questions:

- What is your perspective on the parent advocacy described above? Jot down your immediate impressions.
- What might be some of the intended and unintended consequences of parents' intensive focus on mathematics, as described in the vignettes?

As you may have noticed, these four stories have several commonalities. First, each family has a similar profile. Their incomes are above the median income for their area, they have at least a college degree, and many have master's degrees and doctorates. Likewise, parents are more likely to hold high paying jobs with flexibility in time off. These schools are also located in communities with median incomes approximately double that for their state and the populations consist of primarily white, Asian, or multiracial people. Lastly, every parent in these examples is attentive to and invested in their child's education because they want their children to succeed at life and they share similar ideas of what educational success should look like.

These parents' socioeconomic status confers advantage. Moreover, their advantage does not emerge solely from that individual's work or innate abilities. Advantage is also the result of an individual's belonging to a particular group. Parents with this social identity have the resources to translate their beliefs and goals around education into action by advocating for what they believe will result in the best possible future for their child. The mechanisms which provide advantages are complicated, and varying characteristics, such as those outlined above, (jobs, wages, education, housing, nutritious food, medicine, and cultural definitions) overlap to enhance or diminish a parent's privilege. Therefore, families with a social identity of high socioeconomic status are often, but not always, white and earning a high income. The parenting trends explored in this chapter apply to many, but not all, families with privilege (Lavee and Benjamin, 2015; Luthar et al., 2013).

Although the advocacy around math instruction described above can be intense, math is just one area in which parents hope to "future-proof" their child. Parenting trends vary from region to region and country to country. In the communities above, being "good" at math is a parental focus. In other communities, these areas of attention might include musical skills, proficiency in sports, getting all As, being accelerated or gifted, and more.

Types of advocacies

Parent advocacy among families with high socioeconomic status as their social identity can take two forms. First, parents call upon their substantial resources of money, time, and education to supplement their child's schooling in order to assure their future success. (Romagnoli and Wall, 2012). They regularly assess their child's academic progress and advocate in order to compensate for areas in which they believe their schools are failing. In our vignettes, Ryan, father of two with a doctorate in a STEM field, describes how his peers view the role of mathematics in crafting a child's future. Ryan comments that other parents believe that "the school is not pushing them in the sense that they want [their kids] to achieve academically," and notes that they "feel very strongly about it" (Lee, 2020, p. 117). And so, middle and high school students do elite rhythmic gymnastics while also taking extracurricular math classes, participate in multiple math competitions, travel around the country for team sports, found clubs, take classes over the summer, and more. Such excessive activity leaves students and parents exhausted from playing a "game of academic one-upmanship" (Kohn, 2019, p. 6). In addition to Ryan's observation about his peers, Beth's and Shane's families both dedicate some of their free time to mathematics. Likewise, Ben's family uses their income to enroll him in an after-school mathematics program. This program costs more than $2,000 per year and buys only one hour-long class per week. Moreover, Ben's family must have enough job flexibility to drive him to class every week.

Additionally, parents also advocate for their children within classrooms, schools, and districts. The example of Ginny and Patrick is extreme but demonstrates this type of advocacy. Parents with advantages often advocate for what **their** student needs. Shane's family's finances allow his mother to stay home, and she is able to focus her energy on tailoring his education by providing extra academic instruction and working to change Shane's math instruction at school. In Shane's case, his parents not only believed Shane needed accelerated and traditional instruction in math, but they also believed that all children needed the same. They believed, as a School Committee candidate in Massachusetts asserted, "I know what my child needs and so I know what all children need" (Anonymous, 2021, personal communication, November 1). Of course, anyone working with students and families knows that this is not the case. There is incredible variation among students. This individualist version of advocacy was prevalent during COVID as groups of parents advocated around masking at school, in-person versus remote education, and mandatory vaccines.

These two types of advocacy—supplemental education through parent resources and lobbying schools to meet the specific, perceived needs of their student—are interconnected. When a parent identifies an area of perceived weakness in a school, they may use both approaches interchangeably. Furthermore, one may spark the other. Ginny began by supplementing Shane's learning and moved into lobbying the school. Likewise, a parent who has not been successful at lobbying a school for changes might resort to supplementing their child's education at home. So far, we've seen that families have the resources to advocate through providing supplemental education and by shaping current schooling to their views. But why do families feel this is necessary?

"More is better" advocacy

Another common thread through these stories is the idea that if a student does more, they will have a better future. Ben summarizes this idea simply: "You have to do extra math! If you don't do math you won't get into a good college and if you don't get into a good college, you won't have a good life!" (Lee, 2020, p. 37). Similarly, Beth links math to her future career, even though she is only 12 years old, stating "I love science and I know have to do math but I kinda hate it. And I'm bad at it." And while science and math certainly do go together, Beth's experiences with math have led her to hate it. For Ben and Beth, this means more math outside of the school day and school year. For Shane, more math leads to being ahead of or better than your peers, an advantage to be maintained at any cost—even at the loss of a deeper understanding which creates for him an overwhelming amount of stress at the idea of applying math in any realm beyond a worksheet.

Our vignettes, in line with research, suggest that a "more is better" approach to education may, in fact, be harmful. Ben appears stressed. Beth is missing time with peers and has potentially developed a dislike of math, and Shane has been through four schools in as many years. When you look closely at advocacy among parents with high socioeconomic status and their drive for more education, the "dark side of the family-school relationship" becomes visible (Lareau, 2000, p. 149). Advocating for more education can result in negative unintended consequences for children and their community.

A "'more is better" approach to parenting is not new. In *Unequal Childhoods*, researcher Lareau (2011) describes this approach as "concerted cultivation" noting that middle- and upper-class families, regardless of race, "cultivated" their children (pp. 2–3). Concerted cultivation prioritizes activities which parents perceive will offer their child an advantage over others and choose these activities over other childhood pursuits such as play.

Because parents perceive the stakes to be high and because parents care so deeply for their children, they conclude that if some cultivation is good, then "more must be better." This process requires parents to "take control" of their student's world and dictate it—from academics to extra-curriculars—for success (Reay, 2005, p. 109). This approach is evident in all our vignettes, as parents advocate to create what they consider to be the perfect learning environment for their child.

There are many theories about how a "more is better" belief became common among parents. Some researchers highlight how the reduction of social safety nets such as welfare has signaled to parents that it is not the role of government to support families. Parents are fully responsible for protecting children and no one will help them if something goes wrong (Cooper, 2014). "More is better" parenting has also been reinforced by educational businesses which sell items and services to support parents in meeting their responsibilities. Parents can purchase everything from educational toys, to tutoring services, to college admissions advising, in the hopes of giving their child an edge (Furedi, 2001). Finally, the authors of the *New York Times* opinion piece, *How Entitled Parents Hurt Schools*, argue that "more is better" approaches are one type of "opportunity hoarding" (Lareau et al., 2018). Families with resources use them to launch their children beyond their peers and thus retain their advantages and solidify their status in life.

Whatever the root causes, these ideas have had two important impacts on parent advocacy. First, parents with abundant resources have come to believe that "every child can be a superchild if s/he is exposed to the 'correct' stimulation at the proper developmental moment" (Nadeson, 2002, p. 413); conversely, they believe that if parents fail and get education "wrong," they can permanently damage their child's future. In other words, parent advocacy emerges from parents' belief that their job is to advocate for every need their child has and this intersects with the equally held belief that if their child misses an important educational opportunity, they will never become a fully realized adult. While many parents may hear and believe the myth of the superchild, only families with a high socioeconomic status have the resources to back up their beliefs through advocacy.

Second, advocacy for a child becomes a critical aspect of parenting, one charged with emotion reflecting the supposed urgency of the task. This "sense of urgency and responsibility" (Vincent and Ball, 2007, p. 1061) is a theme running through each vignette. For example, math is critical to having a good life. Beth's parents prioritize math over summer camp. And Ginny's urgency culminates in an attempt to fire a teacher and change a school's math curriculum. Parents with resources end up "weigh[ing] every decision about what their children do in school, or even after school, against the yardstick of what it might contribute to future success" (Kohn, 1998).

Interestingly, the assumptions behind the advocacy work of parents with high socioeconomic identities do not bear out. In fact, research indicates that parenting actions (except in extreme cases) do not significantly impact a child's trajectory, for good or bad (Nadeson, 2002; LeVine and LeVine, 2017). Even so, it is unsurprising that parents who are repeatedly exposed to these ideas through advertisements, media, and their peers feel anxiety about their children's futures. They doubt their ability to successfully shepherd their child into adulthood. It is equally unsurprising that parents with privilege would passionately advocate for the child by using all the resources at their disposal because they believe their actions will make or break their child's future (LeVine and LeVine, 2017). What can teachers, administrators, and staff do to support parents and children with a privileged identity? How can teachers defuse parenting anxiety?

Note Always assess whether parent concerns have merit. Are children in your school system truly lagging in mathematics education? Is this particular child struggling? Are these parents correct? Is there a problem I have missed? If yes—work with the family to meet the child's needs. If no—brainstorm ways to educate this family—and others—teaching and learning in your classroom and school.

Deepen your practice

Reflect on your own upbringing.

- Did your family believe that "more is better" in education? Take a moment to consider and then share your family's perspective on learning.
- Does your current view of education match that of your family? Did your family's belief system support you as a student? Describe the ways it did or did not fit you.

Do families in your current setting subscribe to a "more is better" approach to education?

- List examples and consider why a parent might prioritize that activity for their child. Do you think this approach will be successful? Explain your response.

The unintended consequences of privilege

Contrary to common belief, "more is better" parenting is not always good for children. While some parent attention to and advocacy for learning is positive, there is a "tipping point" after which benefits decrease and adverse outcomes increase (Li, 2014). Moreover, the potential problems created by a "more is better" approach to learning have ramifications for the classroom and school community.

"Elevated maladjustment"

The students in our vignettes range in age from 6 to 12 years old and despite their youth, they do not appear to be happy. Research indicates that children in communities considered to be privileged are at a higher risk for "elevated maladjustment" (Ciciolla et al., 2017; Luthar et al., 2013, p. 1529). Serious, negative behaviors appear in children as young as age 11 and include abuse of alcohol, marijuana, and other drugs, promiscuousness, smoking and vaping, and significant mental health challenges including depression and anxiety (Ciciolla et al., 2017; Li, Obach, and Cheng, 2015; Luthar et al., 2013; Warner, 2005). Unfortunately, these negative outcomes persist into college and are particularly acute in young women due to the stress and anxiety associated with adhering to unrealistic societal images of womanhood (Ciciolla et al., 2017; Luthar et al., 2013). Of course, this outcome does not occur for all children. However, students from high-income communities are at a higher risk than their peers in other social classes (Ciciolla et al., 2017; Luthar et al., 2013).

Ben, Beth, and Shane show hints of these possible negative outcomes. For example, Beth does her math workbook reluctantly, perhaps wishing she could eat lunch and be social with her friends. However, losing summer camp would be too great a blow. Moreover, this pressure may be turning her away from math, instead of toward it. Would Beth voluntarily choose a career in STEM? Ryan's peers barrel ahead with extra math instruction regardless of the impact on their children.

Shane's parents believe him to be gifted in math, but his teacher sees him struggling. He is unable to explain or apply his thinking. Imagine his stress, at age seven, as he tries to reconcile his parents' view of his abilities with his own struggles in class. His stomachaches may be an expression of stress. Moreover, Ginny and Patrick removed Shane from school at the end of the year. This was Shane's fourth school in four years. Each year his parents sought the environment which they believed would best enhance his ability in math, however, each year, he started in a new place with new people, a choice which could potentially have unforeseen consequences on Shane's social world.

This type of parent advocacy not only impacts the children directly involved, it also can have a negative influence on both the classroom and school community. For example, the idea that "more is better" sneaks into common conversation in classrooms, schools, and communities. Ben's assertion that everyone must do extra math outside of school had two impacts on his peers. First, Ben's belief that being good at math is the only path to a good life was introduced and became a topic of conversation among the five- to eight-year-olds in this camp. Second, Ben's introduction of this idea to his fellow students spread performance anxiety beyond Ben's immediate circle. Anecdotally, other students approached their parents and requested to join an extra math program because "all [their] friends are doing it" and they "don't want to fall behind."

Likewise, Ginny rallied the entire first-grade parent community to force a more traditional mathematics curriculum in a private, progressive elementary school. Her advocacy created intense pressure on the teacher, whom she attempted to have fired. Ginny absorbed the time and energy of school administrators by demanding continual meetings. In addition, she generated widespread anxiety among the first-grade parent population, who began to reconsider whether their choice of a progressive setting would damage their children's future opportunities, as asserted by Ginny.

Lastly, a problematic side effect of advocacy for a "more is better" parenting approach is that it may lead to more emphasis on grades than on a child's socioemotional development. For example, at a suburban high school in an affluent community outside Boston, students have their own definitions of grades. An A is "A OK," a B is "bad," and a C is for "community college"—a fate perceived by these students as dreadful. These students believe that grades are inextricably intertwined with their future success and that any one grade can change one's career trajectory. According to a 2014 survey conducted by Making Caring Common, an organization affiliated with Harvard University, reveals that "About 80% of the youth in our survey report that their parents are more concerned about achievement or happiness than caring for others" (Making Caring Common, 2014).

Making Caring Common (2014) surveyed over 10,000 American youth from diverse backgrounds. Their findings indicate that youth, regardless of family income, are receiving a message that their own success is more important than caring for others. That said, youth from families with privileged social identities have parents with the resources to take their vision of academic success and implement it. As a result, "many children in affluent and middle-class communities feel fierce, debilitating pressure to achieve at high levels, resulting in a range of emotional, ethical, and behavioral troubles" (p. 11). Moreover, data indicates that "the focus on happiness, and the focus on achievement in affluent communities, doesn't appear to increase either children's achievement or their happiness" (p. 2) and this pressure appears to "undermine empathy" in children. Overall, this focus may create more problems because students who value accomplishment above community may both create and contribute to a hostile learning environment.

Deepen your practice

- Using the vignettes above, brainstorm ways in which you could educate parent populations about the negative side of parent advocacy. How might you share this information in a compassion manner which recognizes the underlying anxiety parents have about their children's futures?
- Socioemotional learning is critical to future success.
    o How does your setting address SEL needs?
    o How is it implemented?
    o Analyze your setting's program by answering the following questions:

- Is the implementation consistent withing the classroom? Across the school?
- What evidence do you see the students are absorbing and using these ideas?
- Are there areas in which SEL learning conflicts with the advocacy of high socioeconomic status of parents? If so, describe.

Chapter discussion questions

Respond to the parent advocacy statements below:

o My child is ahead of the class in math/reading/science. He/she/they need more to challenge them.
o He/she/they didn't do it and they promise not to do it again. They don't need this punishment—this punishment is not appropriate. I will email the principal, superintendent, state leaders.
o My child needs more homework after school, otherwise they will never learn how to function in an adult world.
o If everyone else gets special treatment, that makes the SAT unfair for my daughter.

- A seventh-grade student aced her Mandarin test. Thrilled and proud, she snapped a photo and texted it to her dad with the comment, "Look! 100%!!!!!" After a bit, her father responded, "Great, now do it in math." What is going on here? How might this student respond? What would you want this parent to know?

Extension activity

Focus on a student in your current class or placement or use one of the examples above. Write out the primary concern a parent has about their child. You might have written, "Ginny believes Shane is gifted and wants him to receive advanced instruction in math."

- Break down this concern. What fundamental concerns does this parent have? What might they misunderstand about teaching and learning at this age?
- Describe how you would address this issue.

Conclusion

Final reflections on parent advocacy: issues of urgency and possibility

What follows are brief reflections on key elements of parent advocacy and social identity. What can we learn from reflecting on parent advocacy broadly? Let's return to Joe, Ada, and Mandy from the Introduction. We know that each of these parents care deeply for their children and want the best for them—in school and in life. However, their stories demonstrate that not all parent concerns are equally urgent. Some parents advocate around problems with serious short- and long-term consequences. And some parents advocate because of an issue attached to their, and/or their child's, social identity. Joe's, Ada's, and Mandy's vignettes have different levels of urgency. Joe and Ada were facing substantial problems with a likelihood of long-term damage.

Urgency, as a theme, is woven through each chapter. Ada, in the Introduction, worked to alleviate the negative impact of long-term bullying on her daughter's mental health. Emily, in Chapters 1 and 2, stood firm against reducing her son Lewis's struggles in school to a behavioral problem based on a racial stereotype, rather than ADHD. The fundamental concern for Emily was the impact on Lewis's emotional well-being and education. After all, what impact would a behavioral adjustment plan have on a child who needed support and accommodations for something else entirely?

Likewise, Eve and Ms Shah, in Chapter 2, worked together to rapidly put a plan in place for Toby. Without this partnership, Toby would have foundered for months until his official IEP, addressing his autism, was in effect. In that case, Toby would have not only lost educational opportunities, but he could potentially have suffered socially and emotionally, as a result of a teacher responding to his needs reactively rather than proactively. Moreover, the rest of his class would have experienced disruptions.

Alex, Willa, and Rich, in Chapter 3 also came face to face with an urgent dilemma. Alex was managing at school. He made it through the day, but only when he made concessions. He avoided using the bathroom, he avoided students who bullied him, and his peers avoided him. These elements created a hostile environment. Alex was forced to focus on surviving an environment which did not meet his physical needs or protect him emotionally. This left very little energy to focus on schoolwork or other typical high school activities, like socializing and joining clubs.

Contrast these stories to those of Mandy, Ginny, and Patrick. Although Mandy was deeply worried about her daughter's math instruction and wanted her child to be successful, it was not clear that Mandy's daughter was, in fact, having problems. Mandy's concerns were located more than ten years in the future. At that moment, her daughter was not in danger physically or emotionally. And yet, Mandy was able to garner attention to her concerns within a month.

Similarly, in Chapter 4, Ginny and Patrick were searching for the perfect educational environment for Shawn. For them, this was defined as a setting which would push Shawn to the edge of his mathematics abilities—abilities which were defined, not by the teacher with 10 years' experience, but by Ginny and Patrick's vision of what Shawn "should" be able to do. Like Mandy, Ginny and Patrick were able to loop other first-grade parents into dissatisfaction by orchestrating meetings and planning ways to force Shawn's teacher, Elsie, into changing her mathematics curriculum. Ultimately, they brought their concerns to the head of school in an attempt to force Elsie into compliance. They did not succeed. However, Ginny and Patrick, like Mandy, were able to build a sense of urgency around a nonurgent problem, while parents with truly urgent concerns were not.

Happily, as educators we have the capability to support *all* children and families in our classrooms with **all** concerns—urgent and not. We can partner with parents in their quests to make school the best possible experience for their student. This involves making sure that the needs of **all** families and children are heard (Lee, 2020).

The consequences of not being heard, for some children, are severe. For Lewis, his mother Emily's inability to be heard resulted in homeschooling for six months. For Alex, lack of concern caused him to change how much liquid he drank in a day and to alter his bathroom habits. Joseph's teacher, Mrs Jordan, was willing to single him out as an "oddball" and to separate his desk from his peers, but she was unwilling to support him in changing his behavior. In this case, Joseph's mother Cassie was able to use her resources and her education to pressure the school into addressing Joseph's needs.

Other parents do not have the resources to force or support change. Joe, Gail, and Dallas, from the Introduction, are a clear example. Joe and Gail came to my parent literacy lesson because they wanted to support Dallas in school. Through a single assumption about their social identity, I made a serious error. The words "Now you try!" exposed the fact that Joe was unable to read. I imagine that Joe felt judged by me, and by extension, the entire school. I had inadvertently pointed out the most obvious reason why Joe could be ill-equipped to support his son in kindergarten. I say "could" because, to me, that's a superficial way of viewing Joe's situation. One could equally argue that someone struggling to read is the perfect person to support a child struggling to read. As educators, we have the power to make sure families are heard. To my shame, I never followed up with Joe and Gail. I should have.

The book that I have written is, in a sense, the one I wish I had had when I was first teaching. I hope that, by breaking down parent advocacy into its many and complicated pieces, you will be better equipped to handle all variety of parent advocacy you will encounter in your career. We *all* want what is best for children, and parents and educators are bound to disagree at times. I hope these vignettes, the research underlying them, and the discussion questions and extension activities will continue to support you as you build relationships with families. So here is one last extension question, one that launched my fascination with the family-school relationship and one that I still consider.

You are a teacher in a Title I literacy kindergarten in a small, economically depressed city in the northeast. Your parent literacy session has just gone awry. You handed a book to a parent, assuming they could read when in fact, they could not. Reflect on this situation—what could you do to prevent this from happening again? What could you do to bring parents like Joe and Gail (from the Introduction) back into a relationship with the school? What feedback could they offer through their advocacy?

References

Abreu, R.L., Rosenkrantz, J., Ryser-Oatman, S., Rotosky, S. and Riggle, E. (2019) "Parental reactions to transgender and gender diverse children: a literature review," *Journal of GLBT Family Studies*, 15(5), pp. 461–485. Available at: https://doi.org/10.1080/1550428x.2019.1656132.

Anderson, L.R., Hemez, P.F. and Kreider, R.M. (2022) *Living arrangements of children: 2019, U.S. Census Bureau*. Available at: www.test.census.gov/library/publications/2022/demo/p70-174.html (Accessed: December 4, 2022).

APA Dictionary of Psychology: Social identity (no date) *American Psychological Association*. American Psychological Association. Available at: https://dictionary.apa.org/social-identity (Accessed: December 17, 2022).

APA Dictionary of Psychology: Socioeconomic status (no date) *American Psychological Association*. American Psychological Association. Available at: https://dictionary.apa.org/socioeconomic-status (Accessed: December 4, 2022).

ASPE (no date) *HHS Poverty Guidelines for 2022, Office of the Assistant Secretary of Planning and Evaluation (ASPE)*. Available at: https://aspe.hhs.gov/topics/poverty-economic-mobility/poverty-guidelines (Accessed: December 17, 2022).

Baker, A.L. and Soden, L.M. (1998) *The challenges of parent involvement research*. New York: ERIC Clearinghouse on Urban Education.

Baquedano-López, P., Alexander, R.A. and Hernandez, S.J. (2013) "Equity issues in parental and community involvement in schools," *Review of Research in Education*, 37(1), pp. 149–182. Available at: https://doi.org/10.3102/0091732x12459718.

Benson, C. (2022) *Poverty rate of children higher than national rate, lower for older populations*, The United States Census Bureau. Available at: www.census.gov/library/stories/2022/10/poverty-rate-varies-by-age-groups.html (Accessed: December 17, 2022).

Bryk, A.S. and Schneider, R.A. (2004) *Trust in schools: a core resource for improvement*. New York: Russell Sage Foundation.

Bull, B., Byno, L., D'Arrigo, J. and Robertson, J. (2022) "Parents of non-binary children: stories of understanding and support," *Journal of Feminist Family Therapy*, 34(1–2), pp. 125–152. Available at: https://doi.org/10.1080/08952833.2022.2029331.

Bureau, U.S.C. (2021) *US Census Bureau guidance on the presentation and comparison of race and Hispanic origin data*, Census.gov. Available at: www.census.gov/topics/population/hispanic-origin/about/comparing-race-and-hispanic-origin.html (Accessed: January 8, 2023).

Bureau, U.S.C. (no date) *School enrollment*, Explore census data. Available at: https://data.census.gov/table?q=s1401&tid=ACSST1Y2021.S1401 (Accessed: December 4, 2022).

Buren, M.K., Rios, K. and Burke, M.M. (2021) "Advocacy experiences among rural parents of children with disabilities," *Rural Special Education Quarterly*, 41(1), pp. 12–24. Available at: https://doi.org/10.1177/87568705211049337.

Cheadle, J.E. and Amato, P.R. (2011) "A quantitative assessment of Lareau's qualitative conclusions about class, race, and parenting," *Journal of Family Issues*, 32(5), pp. 679–706. Available at: https://doi.org/10.1177/0192513x10386305.

Ciciolla, L., Curlee, A., Karageorge, J., and Luthar, S. (2017) "When mothers and fathers are seen as disproportionately valuing achievements: implications for adjustment among upper middle class youth," *Journal of Youth and Adolescence*, 46(5), pp. 1057–1075. Available at: https://doi.org/10.1007/s10964-016-0596-x.

Comer, J.P. and Haynes, N.M. (1991) "Parent involvement in schools: an ecological approach," *The Elementary School Journal*, 91(3), pp. 271–277. Available at: https://doi.org/10.1086/461654.

Cooper, C.W. (2009) "Parent involvement, African American mothers, and the politics of educational care," *Equity & Excellence in Education*, 42(4), pp. 379–394. Available at: https://doi.org/10.1080/10665680903228389.

Cooper, M. (2014) *Cut adrift*. Oakland: University of California Press.

Creamer, J., Shrider, E., Burns, K. and Chen, F. (2022) *Poverty in the United States: 2021*. rep. United States Census Bureau. Available at: //www.census.gov/content/dam/Census/library/publications/2022/demo/p60-277.pdf (Accessed: January 9, 2023).

Dumais, S.A., Kessinger, R.J. and Ghosh, B. (2012) "Concerted cultivation and teachers' evaluations of students: exploring the intersection of race and parents' educational attainment," *Sociological Perspectives*, 55(1), pp. 17–42. Available at: https://doi.org/10.1525/sop.2012.55.1.17.

Dyrness, A. (2011) *Mothers united: an immigrant struggle for socially just education*. Minneapolis: University of Minnesota Press.

Epstein, J.L. (2011) *School, family, and community partnerships: preparing educators and improving schools*. Boulder, CO: Westview Press.

Ferlazzo, L. (2011) *Involvement or engagement? ASCD*. Available at: www.ascd.org/el/articles/involvement-or-engagement (Accessed: December 5, 2022).

Francis, G.L., Blue-Banning, M., Haines, S., Turnbull, A. and Gross, J. (2016) "Building 'our school': parental perspectives for building trusting family–professional partnerships," *Preventing school failure: alternative education for children and youth*, 60(4), pp. 329–336. Available at: https://doi.org/10.1080/1045988x.2016.1164115.

Furedi, F. (2001) *Paranoid parenting: abandon your anxieties and be a good parent*. London, UK: Allen Lane.

Gandara, P.C. and Contreras, F. (2009) *The Latino education crisis: the consequences of failed social policies*. Cambridge, MA, MA: Harvard University Press.

Garey, J. (2022a) *How to support kids who are questioning, Child Mind Institute*. Child Mind Institute. Available at: https://childmind.org/article/how-to-support-kids-who-are-questioning/ (Accessed: December 5, 2022).

Garey, J. (2022b) *Mental health challenges of LGBTQ+ kids, Child Mind Institute*. Child Mind Institute. Available at: https://childmind.org/article/mental-health-challenges-of-lgbtq-kids/ (Accessed: December 5, 2022).

Geller, J.D. (2016) *Ensuring that family engagement initiatives are successful, sustainable, and scalable, Voices in Urban Education*. Annenberg Institute for School Reform at Brown University. Brown University. Available at: https://eric.ed.gov/?id=EJ1110964 (Accessed: December 5, 2022).

Gray, S.A., Sweeney, K., Randazzo, R. and Levitt, H. (2015) "'Am I doing the right thing?': pathways to parenting a gender variant child," *Family Process*, 55(1), pp. 123–138. Available at: https://doi.org/10.1111/famp.12128.

Green, E. (2014) "Why do Americans stink at math?," *The New York Times*, July 27. Available at: https://www.nytimes.com/2014/07/27/magazine/why-do-americans-stink-at-math.html?_r=0 (Accessed: December 4, 2022).

Guzman, G. (2022) *Household income: 2021 – census.gov, US Census Bureau*. Available at: www.census.gov/content/dam/Census/library/publications/2022/acs/acsbr-011.pdf (Accessed: December 4, 2022).

Hart, A. (2019) "Texas ended its special education cap in 2017, but the policy has had long-lasting effects," *Texas Standard*, November 5. Available at: www.texasstandard.org/stories/texas-ended-its-special-education-cap-in-2016-but-the-policy-has-had-long-lasting-effects/ (Accessed: December 4, 2022).

Hill, N. and Taylor, L. (2004) *Parental school involvement and children's academic achievement* ... Sage Journals. Available at: https://journals.sagepub.com/doi/10.1111/j.0963-7214.2004.00298.x (Accessed: December 15, 2022).

Hong, S. (2011) *A cord of three strands: a new approach to parent engagement in schools.* Cambridge, MA: Harvard Education Press.

Horvat, E. M., Weininger, E., and Lareau, A. (2003) "From social ties to social capital: class differences in the relations between schools and parent networks," American Educational Research Association 40(2), pp. 319-351.

Human Rights Campaign (no date) *A parent's quick guide for in-school transitions, Human Rights Campaign.* Available at: www.hrc.org/resources/a-parents-quick-guide-for-in-school-transitions-empowering-families-and-schools-to-support-transgender-and-non-binary-students (Accessed: December 5, 2022).

Ishimaru, A.M. and Lott, J. (2015) *Charting a course to equitable collaboration: learning from parent engagement initiatives in the road map project, Charting a course to equitable collaboration: learning from parent engagement initiatives in the road map project.* University of Washington. Available at: www.education.uw.edu/epsc/files/2015/08/EquitableCollaborationReport_0.pdf (Accessed: December 2022).

Jones, N., Marks, R., Ramirez, R. and Rios-Vargas, M. (2021) *2020 census illuminates racial and ethnic composition of the country, Census.gov.* Available at: www.census.gov/library/stories/2021/08/improved-race-ethnicity-measures-reveal-united-states-population-much-more-multiracial.html (Accessed: December 2022).

Kohn, A. (2019) *Only for my kid: how privileged parents undermine school reform, Alfie Kohn.* Available at: www.alfiekohn.org/article/kid/ (Accessed: December 6, 2022).

Lareau, A. (2000) *Home advantage: social class and parental intervention in elementary education.* Lanham: Rowman & Littlefield.

Lareau, A. (2011) *Unequal childhoods: class, race, and family life.* Berkeley: University of California Press.

Lareau, A. and Horvat, E.M.N. (1999) "Moments of social inclusion and exclusion race, class, and cultural capital in family-school relationships," *Sociology of Education*, 72(1), pp. 37–53. Available at: https://doi.org/10.2307/2673185.

Lareau, A. and Muñoz, V.L. (2012) "You're not going to call the shots: structural conflicts between the principal and the PTO at a suburban public elementary school," *Sociology of Education*, 85(3), pp. 201–218. Available at: https://doi.org/10.1177/0038040711435855.

Lareau, A. and Shumar, W. (1996) "The problem of individualism in family-school policies," *Sociology of Education*, 69, p. 24. Available at: https://doi.org/10.2307/3108454.

Lareau, A., Weininger, E.B. and Cox, A.B. (2018) "Parental challenges to organizational authority in an elite school district: the role of cultural, social, and symbolic capital," *Teachers College Record: The Voice of Scholarship in Education*, 120(1), pp. 1–46. Available at: https://doi.org/10.1177/016146811812000106.

Lavee, E. and Benjamin, O. (2015) "Working-class mothers' school involvement: a class-specific maternal ideal?," *The Sociological Review*, 63(3), pp. 608–625. Available at: https://doi.org/10.1111/1467-954x.12253.

Lee, E.D. (2020) *Win the game or build decent humans? Parental perceptions of the family school-relationship across socioeconomic backgrounds*, DigitalCommons@Lesley. Available at: https://digitalcommons.lesley.edu/education_dissertations/172/ (Accessed: December 11, 2022).

LeVine, R.A. and LeVine, S. (2017) *Do parents matter?: why Japanese babies sleep soundly, Mexican siblings don't fight, and American families should just relax*. London: Souvenir Press.

Li, A. (2014) *How much is too much? Debunking the effects of parental over-involvement at home*, OpenCommons@UConn. Available at: https://opencommons.uconn.edu/gs_theses/681/ (Accessed: December 6, 2022).

Li, A., Obach, H. and Cheng, S. (2015) "How much is too much? Debunking the effects of parental over-involvement at home," American Sociological Association Annual Meeting, 20 August. Chicago: American Sociological Association.

Loftus, Y. (2021) *Autism language: person-first or identity-first?, Autism Parenting Magazine*. Available at: www.autismparentingmagazine.com/autism-language-person-first/ (Accessed: December 4, 2022).

Lopez, G. (2001) "The value of hard work: lessons on parent involvement from an (im)migrant household," *Harvard Educational Review*, 71(3), pp. 416–438. Available at: https://doi.org/10.17763/haer.71.3.43x7k542x023767u.

Love, H.R., Nyegenye, S., Wilt, C. and Annamma, S. (2021) "Black families' resistance to deficit positioning: addressing the paradox of black parent involvement," *Race Ethnicity and Education*, 24(5), pp. 637–653. Available at: https://doi.org/10.1080/13613324.2021.1918403.

Lucas, J. (no date) *Institutionalized bias, Encyclopaedia Britannica*. Encycloaedia Britannica, inc. Available at: www.britannica.com/topic/institutionalized-bias (Accessed: December 17, 2022).

Luelmo, P. and Kasari, C. (2021) "Randomized pilot study of a special education advocacy program for Latinx/minority parents of children with autism spectrum disorder," *Autism*, 25(6), pp. 1809–1815. Available at: https://doi.org/10.1177/1362361321998561.

Luthar, S.S., Barkin, S.H. and Crossman, E.J. (2013) "'I can, therefore I must': fragility in the upper-middle classes," *Development and Psychopathology*, 25(4pt2), pp. 1529–1549. Available at: https://doi.org/10.1017/s0954579413000758.

Making Caring Common (2014) *The children we mean to raise: the real messages adults are sending about values*. rep. Available at: https://mcc.gse.harvard.edu/reports/children-mean-raise.

Mapp, K.L. and Kuttner, P.J. (2013) *Partners in education: a dual capacity-building framework for family-school partnerships*, SEDL. SEDL. Available at: https://eric.ed.gov/?id=ED593896 (Accessed: December 5, 2022).

Marchand, A.D., Vassar, R., Diemer, M. and Rowley, S. (2019) "Integrating race, racism, and critical consciousness in black parents' engagement with schools," *Journal of Family Theory & Review*, 11(3), pp. 367–384. Available at: https://doi.org/10.1111/jftr.12344.

Massachusetts Department of Elementary and Secondary Education (2022). Direct Special Education Expenditures, FY08 to FY21 [Microsoft Excel spreadsheet]. Malden, MA: Massachusetts Department of Elementary and Secondary Education. Available from: www.doe.mass.edu/finance/statistics/ (Accessed: December 13, 2022).

Miller, C. (2022) *Transgender kids and gender dysphoria*, Child Mind Institute. Available at: https://childmind.org/article/transgender-teens-gender-dysphoria/ (Accessed: December 5, 2022).

Mueller, T.G., Singer, G.H. and Draper, L.M. (2008) "Reducing parental dissatisfaction with special education in two school districts: implementing conflict prevention and alternative dispute resolution," *Journal of Educational and Psychological Consultation*, 18(3), pp. 191–233. Available at: https://doi.org/10.1080/10474410701864339.

Nadesan, M.H. (2002) "Engineering the entrepreneurial infant: brain science, infant development toys, and governmentality," *Cultural*

Studies, 16(3), pp. 401–432. Available at: https://doi.org/10.1080/09502380210128315.

National PTA (no date) *A parent's dictionary – special needs guide: National PTA, National Parent Teacher Association*. Available at: www.pta.org/home/family-resources/Special-Education-Toolkit/A-Parents-Dictionary#S (Accessed: December 6, 2022).

NCES (2022) *Students with disabilities, National Center for Education Statistics*. National Center for Education Statistics. Available at: https://nces.ed.gov/programs/coe/indicator/cgg (Accessed: December 6, 2022).

NCES (no date) *Fast facts: back-to-school statistics, National Center for Education Statistics (NCES) Home Page, a part of the US Department of Education*. National Center for Education Statistics. Available at: https://nces.ed.gov/fastfacts/display.asp?id=372 (Accessed: January 9, 2023).

Orr, A. and Baum, J. (no date) *Schools in transition: a guide for supporting transgender students in K-12 schools*. Edited by B. Sherouse. HRC Foundation. Available at: https://hrc-prod-requests.s3-us-west-2.amazonaws.com/Blueprint-2020.pdf?mtime=20201110185320&focal=none (Accessed: December 5, 2022).

Reay, D. (2005) "Doing the dirty work of social class? Mothers' work in support of their children's schooling," *The Sociological Review*, 53(2_suppl), pp. 104–115. Available at: https://doi.org/10.1111/j.1467-954x.2005.00575.x.

Rich, D. (1987) *Schools and families: issues and actions*. Washington, DC: Distributed by ERIC Clearinghouse.

Robinson, K. and Harris, A.L. (2014) *The broken compass: parental involvement with children's education*. Cambridge, MA: Harvard University Press.

Romagnoli, A. and Wall, G. (2012) "'I know I'm a good mom': young, low-income mothers' experiences with risk perception, intensive parenting ideology and parenting education programmes,"

Health, Risk & Society, 14(3), pp. 273–289. Available at: https://doi.org/10.1080/13698575.2012.662634.

Rosenthal, B.M. (2016) "Denied: special ed cap drives families out of public schools," *The Houston Chronicle*, 29 December. Available at: www.houstonchronicle.com/denied/7/ (Accessed: December 4, 2022).

Rothstein, R. (2004) *Class and schools: using social, economic, and educational reform to close the black-white achievement gap*. Washington: Economic Policy Institute.

Samsell, B., Lothman, K., Samsell, E. and Ideishi, R. (2022) "Parents' experiences of caring for a child with autism spectrum disorder in the United States: a systematic review and metasynthesis of qualitative evidence," *Families, Systems, & Health*, 40(1), pp. 93–104. Available at: https://doi.org/10.1037/fsh0000654.

Seager van Dyk, I., Clark, K., Dougherty, L. and Panchankis, J. (2022) "Parent responses to their sexual and gender minority children: implications for parent-focused supportive interventions," *Psychology of Sexual Orientation and Gender Diversity* [Preprint]. Available at: https://doi.org/10.1037/sgd0000589.

Sensoy, Ö. and DiAngelo, R.J. (2017) *Is everyone really equal?: an introduction to key concepts in social justice education*. New York: Teachers College Press.

Shapiro, T.M. (2004) *The hidden cost of being African American: How wealth perpetuates inequality*. Oxford: Oxford University Press.

Sirois, M. (2020) *Not "him" or "her": accepting and loving my non-binary child*, *Scary Mommy*. Scary Mommy. Available at: www.scarymommy.com/accepting-non-binary-gender-nonconfirming-child (Accessed: December 5, 2022).

Stark, C. (2022) "Parent advocacy for transgender and gender-expansive youth," *Journal of Autoethnography*, 3(2), pp. 144–159. Available at: https://doi.org/10.1525/joae.2022.3.2.144.

Strauss, V. (2017) *What the numbers really tell us about America's public schools*, *The Washington Post*. WP Company. Available at: www.washingtonpost.com/news/answer-sheet/wp/2017/03/06/what-the-numbers-really-tell-us-about-americas-public-schools/ (Accessed: December 13, 2022).

Supporting and caring for our gender-expansive youth (no date) *Human Rights Campaign*. Available at: www.hrc.org/supporting-and-caring-for-our-gender-expansive-youth (Accessed: December 5, 2022).

Torres, M.N. and Hurtado-Vivas, R. (2011) "Playing fair with Latino parents as parents, not teachers: beyond family literacy as assisting homework," *Journal of Latinos and Education*, 10(3), pp. 223–244. Available at: https://doi.org/10.1080/15348431.2011.581108.

The Trevor Project (2021) *Understanding gender identities*, *The Trevor Project*. Available at: www.thetrevorproject.org/resources/article/understanding-gender-identities/ (Accessed: December 13, 2022).

The Trevor Project (2022a) *Guide to being an ally to transgender and nonbinary young people*, *The Trevor Project*. The Trevor Project. Available at: www.thetrevorproject.org/resources/guide/a-guide-to-being-an-ally-to-transgender-and-nonbinary-youth/ (Accessed: December 5, 2022).

The Trevor Project (2022b) *Homelessness and housing instability among LGBTQ youth*, *The Trevor Project*. Available at: www.thetrevorproject.org/research-briefs/homelessness-and-housing-instability-among-lgbtq-youth-feb-2022/ (Accessed: December 13, 2022).

Underwood, K. and Killoran, I. (2012) "Parent and family perspectives on engagement: lessons from the early years," *Canadian Journal of Education*, 35(4), pp. 376–414. Available at: https://doi.org/10.32920/ryerson.14636430.

UNICEF (2021) *Nearly 240 million children with disabilities around the world, UNICEF's most comprehensive statistical analysis finds*, *UNICEF*. Available at: www.unicef.org/press-releases/nearly-240-

million-children-disabilities-around-world-unicefs-most-compre hensive (Accessed: December 11, 2022).

US Census Bureau (2021) *US Census Bureau Guidance on the presentation and comparison of race and Hispanic origin data*, Census.gov. Available at: www.census.gov/topics/population/hispanic-origin/about/comparing-race-and-hispanic-origin.html (Accessed: January 8, 2023).

US Census Bureau (2022) *About the topic of race*, The United States Census Bureau. Available at: www.census.gov/topics/population/race/about.html (Accessed: December 13, 2022).

Van Voorhis, F.L. (2011) "Costs and benefits of family involvement in homework," *Journal of Advanced Academics*, 22(2), pp. 220–249. Available at: https://doi.org/10.1177/1932202x1102200203.

Vincent, C. and Ball, S.J. (2007) "'Making up' the middle-class child: Families, activities and class dispositions," *Sociology*, 41(6), pp. 1061–1077. Available at: https://doi.org/10.1177/0038038507082315.

Warner, J.A. (2005) *Perfect madness: motherhood in the age of anxiety*. London: Ebury Digital.

Warren, M.R. and Mapp, K.L. (2011) *A match on dry grass: community organizing as a catalyst for school reform*. Oxford: Oxford University Press.

Williams Institute (2022) *Nonbinary LGBTQ adults in the United States*, Williams Institute. Available at: https://williamsinstitute.law.ucla.edu/publications/nonbinary-lgbtq-adults-us/ (Accessed: December 4, 2022).

Young, J.L., Young, J. and Butler, B.R. (2018) "A student saved is not a dollar earned: a meta-analysis of school disparities in discipline practice toward black children," *Taboo: The Journal of Culture and Education*, 17(4), pp. 94–112. Available at: https://doi.org/10.31390/taboo.17.4.06.

Index

Abreu et al. 76, 78, 80–82, 84
acceptable parent advocacy 30
   gatekeeper or ally? 33
adjusting and adapting 77
advocacy and relationships 54
Alex, Rich, and Willa 73
Angela and Adan 24
APA Dictionary 99

Ben 94
Beth, Rose, and Shawn 95
Bull et al. 66, 76, 78, 82–83, 86–87
Buren, Rios, and Burke 52, 56–57, 60

Cassie and Joseph 48
chapter discussion questions
   ability 63
   high SES 111
   race and ethnicity 39
Cheadle and Amato 12, 93
Ciciolla, Curlee, Karageorge, and Luthar 107
coming out and coming to terms 77

Cooper, C.W. 28, 31, 37

deficit views 27
   gatekeeper or ally? 29
discipline gap 34
   gatekeeper or ally? 35
Dumais, Kessinger, and Ghosh 12, 93

Emily and Lewis 22, 46
Eve and Toby 45
extension activities
   ability 63
   high SES 112
   race and ethnicity 40

final reflections 113

Garey, J. 66, 85
genesis of book 1
Gray et al. 77, 79–80, 85, 87

Hill and Taylor 12, 18, 93
Hong 18

Kit, Geoff, and Leah 70

knowledgeable advocacy 51
Kohn, A. 101, 105

Lareau and Shumar 12, 93–94
Lareau, A. 15, 93–94, 103–104
Lee, E. 3, 5–6, 12–13, 38, 96, 101–102
LeVine and LeVine 15, 105–106
Li, A. 107
Li, Obach, and Cheng 107
Love et al. 28, 31, 35–36
Luelmo and Kasari 51, 53
Luthar et al. 100, 107

Making Caring Common 109–110
Marchand et al. 28, 30–32, 36
Miller, C 66
more is better advocacy 102

Nadeson, M. 104–105
National Center for Education Statistics (NCES) 43–44

Orr and Baum 67–69

Parent advocacy 5
parent advocacy bind 36
  gatekeeper or ally? 39
parental transformation 81

reflection
  ability 51
  gender identity 76
  high SES 99
  race and ethnicity 27
resources and parent advocacy 59
Robinson and Harris 12, 18, 93
Ryan 97

Samsell et al. 54–55, 62
Seager Van Dyk et al. 66, 76, 81–82
Senosy and Diangelo 91, 98
Shane, Ginny, and Patrick 96
Shapiro, T. 12, 28, 92
Sirois, M. 77
social identities and biases 11
Stark, C. 68–69, 77, 84, 86, 88

Torres and Hurtado-Vivas 28, 31
Trevor Project 68–71, 78
types of advocacies
  high SES 100

unconventional advocacy 37
unintended consequences of privilege 107

vignettes

ability 45
gender identity 70
high socioeconomic status 94
race and ethnicity 22
vocabulary
  ability 50
  gender identity 69
  high SES 98
  race and ethnicity 26

will my child be ok? 85

Young, Young, and Butler 34–35

www.ingramcontent.com/pod-product-compliance
Lightning Source LLC
Chambersburg PA
CBHW070808230426
43665CB00017B/2534